News&
Numbers

News & Numbers

A GUIDE TO REPORTING STATISTICAL CLAIMS AND CONTROVERSIES IN HEALTH AND OTHER FIELDS

Victor Cohn

SENIOR WRITER AND COLUMNIST, FORMER SCIENCE EDITOR,
Washington Post

FOREWORD BY Frederick Mosteller
ROGER I. LEE PROFESSOR EMERITUS OF MATHEMATICAL STATISTICS,
Harvard University

A Project of the Center for Health Communication
Harvard School of Public Health

 IOWA STATE UNIVERSITY PRESS / AMES

Composed by Iowa State University Press
Printed in the United States of America

First edition, 1989

Library of Congress Cataloging-in-Publication Data

Cohn, Victor, 1919–
    News & numbers.

    "A project of the Center for Health Communication, Harvard School of Public Health."
    1. Public health — Statistics. 2. Environmental health — Statistics. 3. Vital statistics. I. Harvard School of Public Health. Center for Health Communication. II. Title. III. Title: News and numbers.
RA407.C64 1989   362.1′021   88–6807
ISBN 0–8138–1442–1
ISBN 0–8138–1437–5 (pbk.)

A Note to Readers

THE rules of statistics are the rules of good thinking, codified. They apply to any kind of reporting in which numbers — stated or implied — are involved: political reporting, science reporting, business, economics, sports, or whatever.

This guide is an attempt to explain the role, logic, and language of statistics, so we reporters can ask better questions about the many alleged facts or findings that rest, or should rest, on some credible numbers. Because this manual began as a project of the Harvard School of Public Health, the reporting of health and the environment is the major example. But the principles and many of the suggested "questions for reporters" can be used by inquiring reporters in any field. They can help you read a scientific report or listen to the conflicting claims of politicians, environmentalists, physicians, scientists, or almost anyone and weigh and explain them. And the final chapter specifically shows how these principles apply in all areas.

VICTOR COHN

Contents

Foreword

REPORTERS play an essential role in communicating science to the public. In common with scientists, they desire accuracy. Although health and medicine provide many exciting stories, the biostatistics that scientists must use in their studies presents special problems for reporters. It gives uncommon and misleading meanings to common words like "significant," "consistent," and "power." Mathematical statistics often produces results that are disturbingly counterintuitive, at least at first, to laymen and scientists alike. In vital statistics and epidemiology, definitions often seem arbitrary, and slight changes make considerable differences in the findings.

Science writers often take short courses in special topics such as biostatistics. I have taught in some of these courses and have been impressed by the seriousness of the participants. Nevertheless, they need some of this material in an accessible and permanent form.

Victor Cohn of the *Washington Post* has prepared this manual to help all reporters cut through these statistical tangles. He wants to give them a guide to the ways that statistics can clarify facts or mystify the reader.

Cohn's book grew out of the Media Project of our Health Science Policy Working Group of the Division of Health Policy Research and Education at Harvard University. I am pleased that faculty members of the Harvard School of Public Health have been able to help him produce this book as a visiting fellow

in 1978 and 1984 and as a contributor to the Health Science
Policy Working Group.

Through the Media Project, with the help of Jay Winsten,
we have also examined sources of pressures on the science
writer.[1] In the future we want to use what we have learned
through many discussions with science writers to advise scientists on their role in the media.

By such efforts, including this book, and by many similar
efforts in this and other fields, scientists and writers may gradually upgrade the whole communication system, scientific and
journalistic. Thus we may clear the communication channel
between science and the public.

FREDERICK MOSTELLER

Acknowledgments

My main mentor and guide in the preparation of this book has been Dr. Frederick Mosteller, Roger I. Lee professor emeritus of mathematical statistics and former chairman of the departments of Biostatistics and Health Policy and Management, Harvard School of Public Health. He gave so fully of his time, energy, and knowledge that he should be listed as coauthor but for the fact that I sometimes used a journalist's freewheeling approach rather than a statistician's rigor. This makes any misstatements mine.

The project was supported by the Russell Sage Foundation, and by the Council for the Advancement of Science Writing, which pointed the way in holding seminars on statistics for journalists, including the first of its kind in 1964.

I did much of the work as a visiting fellow at the Harvard School of Public Health, where Dr. Jay Winsten, director of the Center for Health Communication, was another indispensable guide, and Drs. John Bailar III, Nan Laird, Philip Lavin, Thomas A. Louis, and Marvin Zelen were valuable helpers. As were Drs. Gary D. Friedman and Thomas M. Vogt of the Kaiser organizations, Michael Greenberg of Rutgers University, and Peter Montague of Princeton University (on all of whose writings I leaned); Lewis Cope of the Minneapolis *Star Tribune;* Cass Peterson of the *Washington Post;* and my daughter, Deborah Runkle, no mean statistician.

I also owe thanks to Harvard's Drs. Peter Braun, Harvey

Fineberg, Howard Frazier, Howard Hiatt, William Hsaio, Herb Sherman, and William Stason. And to Drs. Stuart A. Bessler, Syntex Corporation; H. Jack Geiger, City University of New York; Nicole Schupf Geiger, Manhattanville College; Charles Moertel, Mayo Clinic; Arnold Relman, *New England Journal of Medicine;* Eugene Robin, Stanford University; and Sidney Wolfe, Public Citizen Health Research Group. Also Katherine Wallman, Council of Professional Associations on Federal Statistics; Howard L. Lewis, American Heart Association; Philip Meyer, University of North Carolina; Mildred Spencer Sanes; Earl Ubell, WCBS-TV, New York City; and Philip Hilts, Cristine Russell, and Barry Sussman, *Washington Post.* I am indebted to my editors at the *Washington Post,* particularly Abigail Trafford, Ben Cason, Carol Krucoff, Len Downie, and Howard Simons for their understanding and support.

The work was also aided by the Andrew W. Mellon Foundation. The American Cancer Society, American Heart Association, Commonwealth Fund, Gannett Foundation, Henry J. Kaiser Family Foundation, Mayo Medical Resources, Milbank Memorial Fund, Pew Charitable Trusts, Philip L. Graham Fund, Russell Sage Foundation, and John Cowles, Jr., have contributed to this manual's initial distribution.

News &
Numbers

Facts and Figures — We Can Do Better

Facts and Figures! Put 'em Down!

> — Charles Dickens (in *The Chimes*)

There are lies, there are damned lies, and there are statistics.

> — Disraeli

Almost everyone has heard that "figures don't lie, but liars can figure." We need statistics, but liars give them a bad name, so to be able to tell the liars from the statisticians is crucial.

> — Dr. Robert Hooke

WE journalists like to think we deal mainly in facts and ideas, but much of what we report is based on numbers.

Politics comes down to votes. Budgets and dollars dominate government. The economy, business, employment, sports—all demand numbers.

The environment, pollutants, toxic chemicals. Again, we see counts and measurements and, most likely, widely varying estimates, some careful, some questionably high or low. An environmentalist says a nuclear power plant or toxic waste dump will cause so many cases of cancer. An industry spokesman denies it. What are their numbers? Where did they get them? How valid are they?

A doctor reports a promising, even exciting new treatment. Is the claim justified or based on a biased or unrepresentative sample? Or too few patients to justify any claim? Science, medicine, technology, the weather, intelligence—all are statistical.

Science is observation, experimentation, measurement, and all these involve numbers, whether we reporters pay attention to them or not.

Statistics are used or misused even by people who tell us, "I don't believe in statistics," then claim that all of us or most people or many do such and such. The question for reporters is, how should we not merely repeat such numbers, stated or implied, but also interpret them to deliver the best possible picture of reality?

We can be better reporters if we understand how the best statisticians—the best figurers—figure. And if we learn a few questions to help us separate the wheat from the chaff.

I do not say that telling the truth—describing reality—will then become easy, for we are constantly bombarded with sweeping claims in convincing wrappings, and the disputed subjects are endless. Medical and surgical treatments, radiation, pesticides, nuclear power, the probability of environmental disasters, the side effects of medicines—almost nothing seems settled.

Like it or not, we must wade in. Whether we will it or not, we have in effect become part of the regulatory apparatus. Dr. Peter Montague of Princeton University tells us, "The environmental and toxic situation is so complex, we can't possibly have enough officials to monitor it. Reporters help officials decide where to focus their activity."

"Journalists opened up" the Love Canal toxic waste issue by "independent investigation," according to Cornell University's Dr. Dorothy Nelkin. "The extensive press coverage contributed to investigations that eventually forced the re-staffing of the Environmental Protection Agency and the creation of a national toxic waste disposal program."[1]

That very coverage, however, may also have stampeded public officials into hasty, ill-conceived studies that left unanswered the crucial question: Did the Love Canal wastes actually cause birth defects and other physical problems?[2] The very way we report a medical or environmental controversy can affect the outcome. If we ignore a bad situation, the public may suffer. If we write "danger," the public may quake. If we write "no danger," the public may be falsely reassured. If we paint an experimental medical treatment too brightly, the public is given false hope.

It is not just what we write, it is what we emphasize. A National Cancer Institute survey indicated that many persons refuse to consider healthy changes in life-style because they think "carcinogens are everywhere in the environment." Such persons probably have read or heard again and again that most cancers are environmentally related, although in the opinion of most informed scientists, most fatal "environmental" cancers are related mainly to individual behavior, outstandingly smoking, and very possibly diet. By various estimates, perhaps 5 to 15 percent of all cancers are related to exposures to man-made carcinogens—chemicals we have inserted into the workplace, foods, air, and water.[3]

When it comes to such emotionally charged and complex issues, or when it simply comes to running for page one or making the six o'clock news, the best among us sometimes overstate or understate. Philip Meyer, veteran reporter and author of *Precision Journalism,* writes, "Journalists who misinterpret statistical data usually tend to err in the direction of overinterpretation. . . . The reason for this professional bias is self-evident; you usually can't write a snappy lead upholding [the negative]. A story purporting to show that apple pie makes you sterile is more interesting than one that says there is no evidence that apple pie changes your life."[4]

We also work fast, sometimes too fast, with severe limits on the space or time we may fill. We find it hard to tell editors or news directors, "I haven't had enough time. I don't have the story yet." Even a long-term project or special may be hurriedly done. In a newsroom "long-term" may mean a few weeks. A major southern newspaper had to print a long, front-page retraction after a series of front-page stories alleged that people who worked at or lived near a plutonium plant suffered in excess numbers from a blood disease. "Our reporters obviously had confused statistics and scientific data," the editor admitted. "We did not ask enough questions."[5]

We tend to oversimplify. We may report, "A study showed that black is white" or "So-and-so announced that . . . ," when a study merely suggested that there was some evidence that such might be the case. We may slight or omit the fact that a scientist calls a result "preliminary." As scientific unsophisticates, we may confuse a study that merely suggests a hypothesis that should be investigated—very frequently the case—with a study that presents strong and conclusive evidence.

We often omit essential perspective, context, or background. Dr. Thomas Vogt of the Kaiser Permanente Center for Health Research tells of seeing the headline "Heart Attacks From Lack of 'C'" and then, two months later, "People Who Take Vitamin C Increase Their Chances of a Heart Attack."[6] Both stories were based on limited, and far from conclusive, animal studies.

Scientists who do poor studies or overstate their results deserve part of the blame. But bad science is no excuse for bad journalism. We tend to rely most on "authorities" who are either most quotable or quickly available or both, and they often tend to be those who get most carried away with their sketchy and unconfirmed but "exciting" data—or have big axes to grind, however lofty their motives. The cautious, unbiased scientist who says, "Our results are inconclusive" or "We don't have enough data yet to make any strong statement" or "I don't know" tends to be omitted or buried someplace down in the story.

We are influenced too by intense and growing competition to tell the story first and tell it most dramatically. I was once asked by a Harvard researcher, "Does competition affect the way you present a story?" I thought and had to answer, "We have to almost overstate. We have to come as close as we can within the boundaries of truth to a dramatic, compelling statement. A weak statement will go no place." Another reporter said, "The fact is, you are going for the strong [lead and story]. And, while not patently absurd, it may not be the lead you would go for a year later."[7]

We reporters are also subject to human hope and human fear. A new "cure" comes along, and we want to believe it. A new alarm is sounded, and we too tremble. Alarms also make news. We too often obey a sardonic maxim: Bad news is good news; good news is no news. Dr. H. Jack Geiger, a respected former science writer and now a professor of medicine, says,

I know I wrote stories in which I explained or interpreted the results wrongly. I wrote stories that didn't have the disclaimers I should have written. I wrote stories under competitive pressure, when it became clear later that I shouldn't have written them. I wrote stories when I hadn't asked—because I didn't know enough to ask—'Was your study capable of getting the answers you wanted? Could it be interpreted to say something else? Did you take into account possible confounding factors?'

How can we learn to do better?

The Certainty
of Uncertainty

2

Too much of the science reporting in the press [blurs] what we're sure of and what we're not very sure of and what is inconclusive. The notion of tentativeness tends to drop out of much reporting.

— Dr. Harvey Brooks

The only trouble with a sure thing is the uncertainty.

— Author unknown

THE first thing to understand about science is that it is almost always uncertain. A scientist, seeking to explain or understand something—be it the behavior of an atom or the effect of the toxic chemicals at a Love Canal—usually proposes a hypothesis, then seeks to test it by experiment or observation. If the evidence is strongly supportive, the hypothesis may then become a theory or at some point even a law, like the law of gravity.

A theory may be so solid that it is generally accepted. Example: the theory that cigarette smoking causes lung cancer, for which almost any reasonable person would say the case has been proved, for all practical purposes. The phrase "for all practical purposes" is important, for scientists, being practical people, must often speak at two levels: the strictly scientific level and the level of ordinary reason that we require for daily guidance.

Example: In June 1985, 16 forensic experts examined the bones that were supposedly those of the "Angel of Death," Dr. Josef Mengele. Dr. Lowell Levine, delegated by the Department of Justice, then said, "The skeleton is that of Josef

Mengele within a reasonable scientific certainty," and Dr. Marcos Segre of the University of Sao Paulo, explained, "We deal with the law of probabilities. We are scientists and not magicians." Pushed by reporters' questions—after all, this was an important matter, and what should the public believe?—several of the pathologists said they had "absolutely no doubt" of their findings.[1] (Later evidence made the case even stronger.)

But all any scientist can scientifically say—say with certainty in almost any such case—is, there is a very strong probability that such and such is true.

Widely believed theories or conclusions are often proved wholly or partly wrong. "When it comes to almost anything we say," reports Dr. Arnold Relman, editor of the *New England Journal of Medicine*, "you, the reporter, must realize—and must help the public understand—that we are almost always dealing with an element of uncertainty. Most scientific information is of a probable nature, and we are only talking about probabilities, not certainty. What we are concluding is the best we can do, our best opinion at the moment, and things may be updated in the future."

Example: Until 1980 the American Cancer Society recommended that women have an annual Pap smear to detect cervical cancer. The recommendation was then changed to every three years for many women, after two initial examinations. Statistics had shown that this would be equally effective.[2] The matter is still controversial, and the recommendation has been changed again in the light of new knowledge.

Scientists are often wrong. In science this is not necessarily a failing. When new evidence disproves an old theory, or occasionally shows that some little believed, even kooky notion is right, the scientific method is doing what it should. It is working.

The public, and even some reporters and especially editors, have a hard time understanding these sometimes drastic revisions. We all hear the question, Why do they say one thing today and another thing tomorrow? I was once on a radio talk show discussing unsettled medical controversies when a testy listener phoned in to exclaim, " 'They say' is a damned liar!"

"They" of course may be different theys who arrive at different conclusions about inconclusive evidence in a thousand areas: the role of fats and cholesterol in the diet, the effects of low-level radioactivity, the cause of the extinction of dinosaurs.

Why so much uncertainty? Science is always a continuing story. Nature is complex, and almost all methods of observation and experiment are imperfect. "There are flaws in all studies," says Harvard's Dr. Marvin Zelen.[3] There may be weaknesses, often unavoidable ones, in the way a study is designed or conducted. Observers are subject to human bias and error. Subjects fluctuate. Measurements fluctuate.

Many studies are thus inconclusive, and virtually no single study proves anything. "Fundamentally," writes Dr. Thomas Vogt, "all scientific investigations require confirmation, and until it is forthcoming all results, no matter how sound they may seem, are preliminary."[4]

Medicine, in particular, is full of disagreement and controversy. "No clinical trial is ever perfect," Harvard's Dr. John Bailar observes. Unlike new drugs, medical treatments and tests and surgical operations need not even be subjected to experimental studies before being applied. "Most treatments escape and will continue to escape rigorous evaluation," Bailar says.[5]

The reasons are many: lack of funds to mount enough trials; lack of enough patients at any one center to mount a meaningful trial; the expense and difficulty of doing multicenter trials; the swift evolution and obsolescence of medical techniques; the fact that, with the best of intentions, medical data— histories, physical examinations, interpretations of tests, descriptions of symptoms and diseases— are notoriously inexact and vary from physician to physician; and the serious ethical obstacles to trying a new procedure when an old one is doing some good, or to experimenting on children, pregnant women, or the mentally ill.

While all studies have flaws, some have more flaws than others. Study after study has found that many articles in the most prestigious medical journals are replete with shaky statistics and lack of any explanation of such crucial matters as patients' complications and the number of patients lost to followup. Papers presented at medical meetings, many of them widely reported by the media, are even less reliable. Many papers are mere progress reports on incomplete studies. Some state tentative results that later collapse. Some are given to draw comment or criticism or get others interested in a provocative but still uncertain finding.[6]

The upshot, according to Dr. Gary Friedman of the Kaiser organization's Permanente Medical Group: "Much of health care is based on tenuous evidence and incomplete knowledge. . . . Seemingly authoritative statements and accepted medical doctrines, perpetuated through textbook and lectures, often turn out to be supported by the most meager of evidence, if any can be found."[7]

In general, possible risks tend to be underestimated and possible benefits overestimated. For decades surgeons swore that only a radical mastectomy was the treatment for breast cancer. Only recently were clinical trials mounted to show that less drastic treatments seem equally effective. Prefrontal lobotomy, overstrict bed rest, drugs by the carload — medical history is rich in treatments that were given for years without question or statistically rigorous study, only to be proved wrong and discarded.

Occasionally, unscrupulous investigators falsify their results. More often, they may wittingly or unwittingly play down data that contradict their theories, or they may search out statistical methods that give them the results they want. Before ascribing fraud, says Harvard's Dr. Frederick Mosteller, "keep in mind the old saying that most institutions have enough incompetence to explain almost any results."[8]

So some uncertainty almost always prevails. But uncertainty need not stand in the way of good sense. To live — to survive on this globe, to maintain our health, to set public policy, to govern ourselves — we almost always must act on the basis of incomplete or uncertain information. There is a way we can do so.

The Scientific Way

Somehow the wondrous promise of the earth is that there are things beautiful in it, things wondrous and alluring, and by virtue of your trade, you want to understand them.

> —Mitchell Feigenbaum
> *Cornell University physicist and mathematician*

The great tragedy of Science—the slaying of a beautiful hypothesis by an ugly fact.

> —Thomas Henry Huxley

To reporters, the world is full of true believers, peddling their "truths." The sincerely misguided and the outright fakers are often highly convincing, also newsy. How can we tell the facts, or the probable facts, from the chaff?

We can borrow from science. We can try to judge all possible claims of fact by the same methods and rules of evidence that scientists use to derive some reasonable guidance in scores of unsettled issues.

As a start, we can ask these questions:

How do you know?

Have the claims been subjected to any studies or experiments?

Were the studies acceptable ones, by general agreement? For example: Were they without any substantial bias?

Have results been fairly consistent from study to study?

Have the findings resulted in a consensus among others in the same field? Do at least the majority of informed persons agree? Or should we withhold judgment until there is more evidence?

Always: *Are the conclusions backed by believable statistical evidence?*

And what is the degree of certainty or uncertainty? How sure can you be?

Obviously, much of statistics involves attitude or policy rather than numbers. And much, at least much of the statistics that reporters can most readily apply, is good sense.

There are many definitions of statistics as a tool. A few useful ones: The science and art of gathering, analyzing, and interpreting data; a means of deciding whether an effect is real; a way of extracting information from a mass of raw data; a set of mathematical processes derived from probability theory.

Statistics can be manipulated by charlatans, self-deluders, and inexpert statisticians. Deciding on the truth of a matter can be difficult for the best statisticians, and sometimes no decision is possible. Uncertainty will ever rule in some situations and lurk in almost all.

There are rare situations in which no statistics are needed. "Edison had it easy," says Dr. Robert Hooke, a statistician and author. "It doesn't take statistics to see that a light has come on."[1] It did not take statistics to tell 19th-century physicians that Morton's ether anesthesia permitted painless surgery or to tell 20th-century physicians that the first antibiotics cured infections that until then had been highly fatal.

Overwhelmingly, however, the use of statistics, based on probability, is called the soundest method of decision making, and the use of large numbers of cases, statistically analyzed, is called the only means for determining the unknown cause of many events. Birth control pills were tested on several hundred women, yet the pills had to be used for several years by millions before it became unequivocally clear that some women would develop heart attacks or strokes. The pills had to be used for some years more before it became clear that the greatest risk was to women who smoked and women over 35.

The best statisticians, let alone practitioners on the firing line (for example, physicians), often have trouble deciding when a study is adequate or meaningful. Most of us cannot become statisticians, but we can at least learn that there are studies and studies, and the unadorned claim "We made a study" or "We did an experiment" may not mean much. We can learn to ask more pointed questions if we understand some basic concepts and other facts about scientific studies.

These are some bedrock statistical concepts:

- Probability
- "Power" and numbers
- Bias and confounders
- Variability

Probability

Scientists cope with uncertainty by measuring probabilities. Since all experimental results and all events can be influenced by chance and almost nothing is 100 percent certain in science and medicine and life, probabilities sensibly describe what has happened and should happen in the future under similar conditions. Aristotle said, "The probable is what usually happens," but he might have added that the improbable happens more often than most of us realize.

The accepted numerical expression of probability in evaluating scientific and medical studies is the *P* (or *probability*) value. The *P* value is one of the most important figures a reporter should look for. It is determined by a statistical formula that takes into account the numbers of subjects or events being compared in order to answer the question, could a difference or result this great or greater have occurred *by chance alone?* By more precise definition, the *P* value expresses the probability that an observed relationship or effect or result could have *seemed* to occur by chance *if there had actually been no real effect.* A low *P* value means a low probability that this happened, that a medical treatment, for example, might have been declared beneficial when in truth it was not.

Here is why the *P* value is used to evaluate results. A

scientific investigator first forms a hypothesis. Then he or she commonly sets out to try to *disprove* it by what is called the *null hypothesis:* that there is no effect, that nothing will happen. To back the original hypothesis, the results must *reject* the null hypothesis. The *P* value, then, is expressed either as an exact number or as <.05, say, or >.05, meaning "less than" or "greater than" a 5 percent probability that nothing has happened, that the observed result could have happened just by chance—or, to use a more elegant statistician's phrase, by *random variation.*

• By convention, *a P value of .05 or less,* meaning there are only 5 or fewer chances in 100 that the result could have happened by chance, is most often regarded as *low.* This value is usually called *statistically significant* (though sometimes other values are used). The unadorned term "statistically significant" usually implies that *P* is .05 or less.

• *A higher P value,* one *greater than .05,* is usually seen as not statistically significant. The higher the value, the more likely the result is due to chance.

In common language, a low chance of chance alone calling the shots replaces the "it's certain" or "close to certain" of ordinary logic. A strong chance that chance could have ruled replaces "it can't be" or "almost certainly can't be."

Why the number .05 or less? Partly for standardization. People have agreed that this is a good cutoff point for most purposes. And partly out of old friend common sense. Frederick Mosteller tells us that if you toss a coin repeatedly in a college class and after each toss ask the class if there is anything suspicious going on, "hands suddenly go up all over the room" after the fifth head or tail in a row. There happens to be only 1 chance in 16—.0625, not far from .05, or 5 chances in 100— that five heads or tails in a row will show up in five tosses, "so there is some empirical evidence that the rarity of events in the neighborhood of .05 begins to set people's teeth on edge."[2]

Another common way of reporting probability is to calculate a *confidence level,* as well as a *confidence interval* (or *confidence limits* or *range*). This is what happens when a political pollster reports that candidate X would now get 50 percent of the vote and thereby lead candidate Y by 3 percentage points, "with a 3-percentage-point margin of error plus or minus and a 95 percent confidence level." In other words, Mr. or Ms. Pollster is 95 percent confident that X's share of the vote would be someplace between 53 and 47 percent. Similarly, candidate Y's share might be 3 percentage points greater (or less) than the figure predicted. In a close election, that margin of error could obviously turn a predicted defeat into victory. And that sometimes happens.

An important point in looking at the results of political polls (and any other statements of confidence): In the reports we read, the plus or minus 3 (or whatever) percentage points is often omitted, and the pollster merely mentions a "3-point margin of error." This means there is actually a 6-point range within which the truth *probably* lurks.

The more people who are questioned in a political poll or the larger the number of subjects in a medical study, the greater the chance of a high confidence level and a narrow, and therefore more reassuring, confidence interval.

No matter how reassuring they sound, P values and confidence statements cannot be taken as gospel, for .05 is not a guarantee, just a number. There are several important reasons for this.

• All that P values measure is the *probability* that the results might have been produced by some sneaky random process. In 20 results where only chance is at work, 1, on the average, will have a reassuring-sounding but misleading P value of $< .05$. One, in short, may be a false positive.

Dr. Marvin Zelen points out that there may be 6,000 to 10,000 clinical (medical) trials of cancer treatment under way today, and if the conventional value of .05 is adopted as the upper permissible limit for false positives, then every 100 studies with no actual benefit may, on average, produce 5 false-positive results. Hence, we may expect 50 false positive results, on average, for every 1,000 trials with no beneficial effects! Zelen in fact has said, "We may now have reached an impasse in cancer chemotherapy in which there are large numbers of false-positive therapies in the clinic,"[3] leading physicians down many false paths.

Amazingly, most false positives probably remain undetected. Scientists do not profit much professionally by reporting negative results. Journal editors are not keen on publishing them. Nor are scientists keen on doing costly and time-consuming studies that merely confirm someone else's work, so "confirmatory studies are rare," Zelen reports.

• Statistical significance alone does not mean there is a cause and effect. *Correlation* or *association* is not causation. Remember the rooster who thought his crowing made the sun rise? Unless an association is so powerful and so constantly repeated that the case is overwhelming, association is only a clue, meaning more study or confirmation is needed.

To statisticians, incidentally, there is this important difference between correlation and association: *Association* means there is at least a possible relation between two variables. A *correlation* is a measure of the association.

• If the number of subjects is too small, an unimpressive *P* value may simply mean that there were too few subjects to detect something that might have shown an effect in more subjects. Highly "significant" *P* values can sometimes adorn negligible differences in large samples.

• An impressive *P* value might also be explained by some other variable or variables — other conditions or associations — not taken into account.

• Statistical significance does not mean biological, clinical — that is, medical — or practical significance, though inexperienced reporters sometimes see or hear the word "significant" and jump to that conclusion, even reporting that the scientists called their study "significant." Example: A tiny difference between two large groups in mean hemoglobin concentration, or red blood count (say, 0.1 g/100 mL, or a tenth of a gram per 100 milliliters), may be statistically significant yet medically meaningless.[4]

• Eager scientists can consciously or unconsciously manipulate the P value by failing to adjust for other factors, by choosing to compare different end points in a study (say, condition on leaving the hospital rather than length of survival), or by choosing the way the P value is calculated or reported.

There are several mathematical paths to a P value, such as the chi-square (χ^2), t, F, r, and paired t tests. All may be legitimate. But be warned. Dr. David Salsburg of Pfizer, Inc., has written in the *American Statistician* of the unscrupulous practitioner who "engages in a ritual known as 'hunting for P values'" and finds ways to modify the original data to "produce a rich collection of small P values" even if those that result from simply comparing two treatments "never reach the magical .05."[5]

"If you look hard enough through your data," contributes an investigator at a major medical center, "if you do enough subset analyses, if you go through 20 subsets, you can find one" — say, "the effect of chemotherapy on premenopausal women with two to five lymph nodes" — "with a P value less than .05. And people do this."

"Statistical tests provide a basis for probability statements," writes Dr. John Bailar, "only when the hypothesis is fully developed before the data are examined. . . . If even the briefest glance at a study's results moves the investigator to consider a hypothesis not formulated before the study was started, that glance destroys the probability value of the evidence at hand." (At the same time, Bailar adds, "review of data for unexpected clues . . . can be an immensely fruitful source of ideas" for new hypotheses "that can be tested in the correct way." And occasionally "findings may be so striking that independent confirmation . . . is superfluous.")[6]

A rather sophisticated — and possibly touchy — line of questioning that some reporters might want to try if they're skeptical: *How did you arrive at your P value? Did you use the test planned in advance in your protocol or study design, or did you apply several tests, then report the best-sounding one?*

And you may think of other questions.

The laws of probability also teach us to *expect* some unusual, even impossible-sounding events.

We've all taken a trip to New York or London or someplace and bumped into someone from home. The chance of that? I don't know, but if you and I tossed for a drink every day after work, the chance that I would ever win 10 times in a row is 1 in 1,024. Yet I would probably do so sometime in a four- or five-year period. What I like to call the Law of Unusual Events — statisticians call it the Law of Small Probabilities — tells us that a few people with apparently fatal illnesses will inexplicably recover, there will be some amazing clusters of cases of cancer or birth defects that will have no common cause, and I may once in a great while bump into a friend far from home.

In a large enough population such coincidences are not unusual. They are the rule. They produce striking anecdotes and often striking news stories. In the medical world they produce unreliable, though often cited, testimonial or anecdotal evidence. "The world is large," Vogt notes, "and one can find a large number of people to whom the most bizarre events have occurred. They all have personal explanations. The vast majority are wrong."[7]

"We [reporters] are overly susceptible to anecdotal evidence," Philip Meyer writes. "Anecdotes make good reading, and we are right to use them. . . . But we often forget to remind our readers — and ourselves — of the folly of generalizing from a few interesting cases. . . . The statistic is hard to remember. The success stories are not."[8]

A statistic to ask about is the *denominator* — the number of people or, a statistician would say, the *population* or domain — in whom such an event might happen. Zelen cites this example: The chance of any youngster between ages five and nine developing leukemia is 3 in 100,000 per year. In a school with 100 children of this age group, we would expect only 3 cases in 100 years. But in this nation with thousands of schools, we would occasionally—such is chance—find schools with 3 or more cases in a single year. "Then one is faced with the problem of interpretation," Zelen says. "Is this one of those rare events that is surely going to be observed? Or is it due to some causal factor?"

A reporter in this instance might ask a statistician at the National Cancer Institute or a medical center, What is the chance of such an event in such a population? How many similar unusual events are probably never reported?

"Power" and Numbers

This gets us to another statistical concept: *power*. Statistically, "power" means the probability of finding something if it's there. Example: Given that there is a true effect, say a difference between two medical treatments or an increase in cancer caused by a toxin in a group of workers, how likely are we to find it?

Sample size confers power. Statisticians say, "Funny things can happen in small samples without meaning very much" . . . "There is no probability until the sample size is there" . . . "Large numbers confer power" . . . "Large numbers at least make us sit up and take notice."*

All this concern about sample size can also be expressed as the *law of large numbers,* which says that as the number of cases increases, the probable truth of a conclusion or forecast increases. The *validity* (truth or accuracy) and *reliability* (reproducibility) of the statistics begin to converge on the truth.

We already learned this when we talked about probability.

---

*There is another unrelated use of the word "power." Scientists commonly speak of increasing or "raising" some quantity *by a power of* 2 or 3 or 100 or whatever. "Power" here means the product you get when you multiply a number by itself one or more times. Thus, in $2 \times 2 = 4$, 4 is the second power of 2, or to put it another way, there are two 2's in your equation. This is commonly written 2^2 and known as 2 to the second power or just 2 to the second. In $2 \times 2 \times 2 = 8$, 2 has been raised to the third power. When you think about 2^{100}, you see the need for the shorthand.

But by thinking of power as statisticians do—as a function of both sample size and the accuracy of measurement, since that too affects the probability of finding something—we can see that if the number of treated patients is small in a medical study, a shift from success to failure in only a few patients could dramatically decrease the success rate.

If six patients have been treated with a 50 percent success rate, the shift to the failure column of just one would cut the success rate to 33 percent. And the total number is so small in any case that the result has little reliability. The result might be valid or accurate, but it would not be generalizable—it would not have reliability until confirmed by careful studies in larger samples. The larger the sample, and assuming there have been no fatal biases or other flaws, the more confidence a statistician would have in the result.

One canny science reporter, Lewis Cope, says,

I have my own "rule of two." If someone makes some numerical claim, I look at the numbers, then see how much I might change the finding by adding or subtracting two from any of the figures. For example, someone says there are five cases of cancer in a community. Would it seem meaningful if there were three?

Or if there were eight cases this year but four the year before—a 100 percent increase—I ask myself, "If I add two cases to last year's total and subtract two from this year's, is there a chance things haven't changed, except by chance?" This approach will never supplant refined analysis. But by playing around with the numbers this way—I sometimes try three instead of two—a reporter can often spot a potential problem or error.

A statistician says, "This can help with small numbers but not large ones." Mosteller contributes "a little trick I use a lot on counts of any size." He explains, "Let's say some political unit has 10,000 crimes or deaths or accidents this year. Has something new happened? The minimum standard deviation [see page 33] for a number like that is 100 — that is, the square root of the original number. That means the number may vary by a minimum of 200 every year without even considering growth, the business cycle, or any other effect. This will supplement your reporter's approach."

Looking for error in reported results, statisticians try to spot both false positives and false negatives. The *false positive* (or *Type I* or *alpha error* in statistical language you may see) is to find a result or effect where there is none. The *false negative* (or *Type II* or *beta error*) is to miss an effect where there is one. The latter is particularly common when there are small numbers. "There are some very well conducted studies with small numbers, even five patients, in which the results are so clear-cut that you don't have to worry about power," says Dr. Relman. "You still have to worry about applicability to a larger population, but you don't have to doubt that there was an effect. When results are negative, however, you have to ask, How large would the effect have to be to be discovered?"

Many scientific and medical studies are underpowered — that is, they include too few cases. "Whenever you see a negative result," another scientist says, "you should ask, What is the power? What was the chance of finding the result if there was one?" One study found that an astonishing 70 percent of 71 well-regarded clinical trials that reported no effect had too few patients to show a 25 percent difference in outcome. Half of the trials could not have detected a 50 percent difference.[9]

A statistician scanned an article on colon cancer in a leading journal. "If you read the article carefully," he said, "you will see that if one treatment was better than the other — if it would increase median survival by 50 percent, from five to seven and a half years, say — they had only a 60 percent chance of finding it out. That's little better than tossing a coin!"

The weak power of that study would be expressed numerically as .6, or 60 percent. Scan an article's fine print or footnotes, and you will sometimes find such a *power statement*. Most authors still don't report one, but the practice is growing, especially when results are negative.

How large is a large enough sample? One statistician calculated that a trial has to have 50 patients before there is even a 30 percent chance of finding a 50 percent difference in results.

Sometimes large populations indeed are needed.[10] If some kind of cancer usually strikes 3 people per 2,000, and you suspect that the rate is quadrupled in people exposed to substance X, you would have to study 4,000 people for the observed excess rate to have a 95 percent chance of reaching statistical significance. The likelihood that a 30-to-39-year-old woman will suffer a myocardial infarction, or heart attack, while taking an oral contraceptive is about 1 in 18,000 per year. To be 95 percent sure of observing at least one such event in a one-year trial, you would have to observe nearly 54,000 women.[11]

Even the lack of an effect—statistically sometimes called a zero numerator—can be a trap. Say, someone reports, "We have treated 14 leukemic boys for five years with no resulting testicular dysfunction"—that is, zero abnormalities in 14. The question remains, how many cases would they have had to treat to have any real chance of seeing an effect? The probability of an effect may be small yet highly important to know about.

All this means you must often ask, *What's your denominator? What's the size of your population?** A disease rate of 10 percent in 20 individuals may not mean much. A 10 percent rate in 200 persons would be more impressive. A rate is only a figure. Always try to get both the numerator and the denominator.

The most important rule of all about any numbers: Ask for them. When anyone makes an assertion that should include numbers and fails to give them, when anyone says that most people, or even X percent, do such and such, you should ask,

---

*And know that to a statistician a population does not necessarily mean a group of people. Statistically, a *population* is any group or collection of pertinent units—units with one or more pertinent characteristics in common—people, events, objects, records, test scores, or physiological values (like blood pressure readings). Statisticians also use the term *universe* for a whole group of people or units under study.

What are your numbers? After all, some researchers reportedly announced a new treatment for a disease of chickens by saying, "33.3 percent were cured, 33.3 percent died, and the other one got away."

Bias and Confounders

One scientist once said that lefties are overrepresented among baseball's heavy hitters. He saw this as "a possible result of their hemispheric lateralization, the relative roles of the two sides of the brain." A critic who had seen more ball games said some simpler covariables could explain the difference. When they swing, left-handed hitters are already on the move toward first base. And most pitchers are right-handers who throw most often to right-handed hitters.[12]

Scientist A was apparently guilty of *bias,* meaning the introduction of spurious associations and error by failing to consider other influential factors. The other factors may be called *covariables, covariates, intervening* or *contributing variables, confounding variables,* or *confounders.* A simpler term may be "other explanations."

Statisticians call bias "the most serious and pervasive problem in the interpretation of data from clinical trials" . . . "the central issue of epidemiological research" . . . "the most common cause of unreliable data." Able and conscientious scientists try to eliminate biases or account for them in some way. But not everybody who makes a scientific, medical, or environmental claim is that skilled. Or that honest. Or that all-powerful. Some biases are unavoidable by the very difficulty of much research, and the most insidious biases of all, says one statistician, are "those we don't know exist."

Some biases may be uncovered by assiduous investigation. A father noticed that every time one of his 11 kids dropped a piece of bread on the floor, it landed with the buttered side up. "This utterly defies the laws of chance," he exclaimed. Close examination disclosed the cause: The kids were buttering their bread on both sides.

I told this story to one statistician, who said, "I was once called about a person who had won first, second, and third prizes in a church lottery. I was asked to assess the probability that this could have happened. I found out that the winner had bought nearly all the tickets."

He had of course asked the obvious question for both scientist and reporters: *Could the relationship described be explained by other factors?*

Not everyone will tell you, of course, for bias is a pervasive human failing. As one candid scientist is said to have admitted, "I wouldn't have seen it if I hadn't believed it." Enthusiastic investigators often tell us their findings are exciting. But they may be so exciting that the investigators paint the results in over-rosy hues.

Other powerful human drives—the race for academic promotion and prestige, financial connections—can also create conscious or unconscious conflicts of interest or attitudes that feed bias. Dr. Thomas Chalmers of Mount Sinai Medical Center in New York tells of a drug trial, financed by a pharmaceutical firm, in which both the head of the study committee and the main statisticians and analysts were the firm's employees, though not so identified in any credits. He tells of a study of oral drugs for diabetes in which the fact that the first author had previously published 14 articles on the subject, and in 7 had acknowledged support by the drug manufacturers, was "not known to the reader."

In contrast, Chalmers describes a study also financed by a drug firm but with a contract specifying a study protocol designed by independent investigators and monitored by an outside board less likely to be influenced by a desire for a favorable outcome. "It is never possible to eliminate" potential conflicts of interest in biomedical research, he concludes, but they should be disclosed so others can evaluate them.[13]

Even a genius may be biased. Horace Freeland Judson of Johns Hopkins University tells how Isaac Newton experimented with prisms and lenses and developed a theory of color, light, and the solar spectrum. He did not report seeing some dark lines—absorption lines, which mark varying wavelengths—that his instruments must have shown. A modern scientist argues that Newton's theory, not his instruments, had no place for that evidence: "To the observing scientist, hypothesis is both friend and enemy."[14]

For years technicians making blood counts were guided by textbooks that told them two or more "properly" studied samples from the same blood should not vary beyond narrow "allowable" limits. Reported counts always stayed inside those limits. A Mayo Clinic statistician rechecked and found that at least two thirds of the time the discrepancies exceeded the supposed limits. The technicians had been seeing what they had been told to expect and discounting any differences as mistakes. This also saved them from the additional labor of doing still more counting.

Both the *biased observer* and the *biased subject* are common in medicine. A researcher who wants to see a treatment result may see one. A patient may report one out of eagerness to please the researcher. There is also the powerful *placebo effect.* Summarizing many studies, one scientist found that half the patients with headaches or seasickness—and a third of those suffering from coughs, mood changes, anxiety, the common cold, and even the disabling chest pains of angina pectoris—reported relief from a "nothing pill."[15] A placebo is not truly a nothing pill; the mere expectation of relief seems to trigger important effects within the body. But in a careful study the placebo should not do as well as a test medication; otherwise the test medication is no better than a placebo.

Sampling bias is the bugaboo of both political polls and medical studies. Say you want to know what proportion of the populace has heart disease, so you stand on a corner and ask people as they pass. Your sample is biased, if only because it leaves out those too disabled to get around. Your problem, a statistician would say, is *selection.* A political pollster who fails to build a valid probability sample, easy when questioning only a thousand or so people from coast to coast, has equally poor selection.[16]

A doctor in a clinic or hospital with an unrepresentative patient population—healthier or sicker or richer or poorer than average—may report results that do not represent the population as a whole. Veterans Administration hospitals, for example, treat relatively few women; their conclusions may apply only to the disproportionate number of lower-income men who typically seek out the VA hospitals' free care. A celebrated Mayo or Cleveland or Ochsner clinic sees both a disproportionate number of difficult cases and a disproportionate number of patients affluent and well enough to travel. The famed Kinsey reports were valuable revelations of sexual behavior but flawed because the samples consisted disproportionately of upper middle-class men and women and of those willing to talk.

An investigator may also introduce bias by *constraining*, or distorting, a sample—by failing to reveal *nonresponse* or by otherwise "throwing away data." A surgeon cites his success rate in those discharged from the hospital after an operation but omits those who died during or just after the procedure. Many people drop out of studies—sometimes they just quit—or they are dropped for various reasons: They could not be evaluated, they came down with some "irrelevant" disorders, they moved away, they died. In fact, many of those not counted may have had unfavorable outcomes had they stayed in the study.

Mosteller tells of a nationwide study of a possibly dangerous anesthetic. The investigators relied on autopsy results at 38 hospitals. Unfortunately, only about 60 percent of the relevant dead had been autopsied, and "anything could have been explained by the missing 40 percent, so that part of the study wound up with a handful of nothing."

The presence of significant nonresponse can often be detected, when reading medical papers, by counting the number of patients treated versus the number of untreated or differently treated *controls*—patients with whom the treated patients are compared. If the number of controls is strikingly greater in a randomized clinical trial (though not necessarily in an epidemiological or environmental study), there were probably many dropouts. A well-conducted study should describe and account for them. A study that does not may report a favorable treatment result by ignoring the fate of the dropouts—a confounding variable.

Age, gender, occupation, nationality, race, income, socioeconomic status, health status, and powerful behaviors like smoking are all possible confounding—and frequently ignored—variables. In the 1970s, foes of adding fluoride to city water pointed to crude cancer mortality rates in two groups of 10 U.S. cities. One group had added fluoride to water, the other had not, and from 1950 to 1970 the cancer mortality rate rose faster in the fluoridated cities. The National Cancer Institute pointed out that the two groups were not equal: The difference in cancer deaths was almost entirely explained by differences in age, race, and sex. The age-, race-, and sex-adjusted difference actually showed a small, unexplained lower mortality rate in the fluoridated cities.[17]

If you look carefully at the fate of women taking birth control pills, you find that advancing age and smoking are the two great confounders. You must take both into account to find the greatest clusters of ill effects. Smoking has been an important confounder in studies of industrial contaminants like asbestos, in which, again, the smokers suffer a disproportionate number of ill effects.[18]

A 1947 survey of Chicago lawyers showed that those who had mere high school diplomas before entering legal training earned 6.3 percent more, on the average, than college graduates. The confounder here—the real explanation—was age. In 1947 there were still many older lawyers without college degrees, and they were simply older, on the average, and hence more established.[19]

Occupational studies often confront another seeming paradox: The workers exposed to some possible adverse effect turn out to be healthier than a control group of persons without such exposure. The confounder: the well-known *healthy-worker effect.*

Workers tend to be healthier and live longer than the population in general.

Some studies of workers in steel mills showed no overall increase in cancer, despite possible exposures to various carcinogens. It took a look at black workers alone to find excess cancer. They commonly worked at the coke ovens, where carcinogens were emitted. This was a case where the population had to be *stratified*, or broken up in some meaningful way, to find the facts. Such findings in blacks often may be falsely ascribed to race or genetics, when the real or at least the most important contributing or ruling variables—to a statistician, the *independent variables*—are occupation and the social and economic plights that put blacks in vulnerable settings. The excess cancer is the *dependent variable*, the result.

"In a two-variable relationship," Dr. Gary Friedman explains, "one is usually considered the independent variable, which affects the other or dependent variable."[20] Take the fact that more people get colds in winter. Here weather is commonly seen as the underlying or independent variable, which affects incidence of the common cold, the dependent variable. Actually, of course, some people, like children in school who are constantly exposed to new viruses, are more vulnerable to colds than others. In the case of these children, then, as in the case of the black workers at the coke ovens, there is often more than one independent variable. Also, some people think that an important underlying reason for the prevalence of colds in winter may be that children are congregated in school, giving colds to each other, thence to their families, thence to their families' coworkers, thence to the coworkers' families, and so on. But cold weather—and home heating?—may still figure, perhaps by drying nasal passages and making them more vulnerable to viruses.

The search for *true variables* is obviously one of the main pursuits of the epidemiologist, or disease detective—or of any physician who wants to know what has affected a patient, or of any student of society who seeks true causes. Like colds, many medical conditions, such as heart disease, cancer, and probably mental illness, have multiple contributing factors. Where many known, measurable factors are involved, statisticians can use mathematical techniques—the terms you will see include *multiple regression, multivariate analysis,* and *discriminant analysis* and *factor, cluster, path,* and *two-stage least-squares analyses*—to relate all the variables and try to find which are the truly important predictors. Yet some situations, like the striking decline in U.S. heart disease mortality in recent years, defy such analyses. These years have seen several major changes in American life that may play a role: less smoking among men, consumption of a leaner diet, more recreational exercise (though more sedentary work). Medical care is far better, including the treatment of hypertension, which disposes people to heart disease. Many of these variables cannot be well measured, and the effect of some is debatable, so—a common situation in science—the truth remains uncertain.

Variability

Doctors always say, "Most things are better in the morning," and they're mostly right. Most chronic or recurring conditions wax and wane. We tend to wake up at night when the condition is at its worst. Then, no matter what is done by way of treatment the next day, the odds are that we'll feel better.

This is *regression toward the mean:* the tendency of all values in every field of science—physical, biological, social, and economic—to move toward the average. Tall fathers tend to have shorter sons, and short fathers, taller sons. The students who get the highest grades on an exam tend to get somewhat lower ones the next time. The regression effect is common to all repeated measurements.

Regression is part of an even more basic phenomenon: *variation,* or *variability.* Virtually everything that is measured varies from measurement to measurement. When repeated, every experiment has at least slightly different results. Take a patient's blood pressure, pulse rate, or blood count several times in a row, and the readings will be somewhat different. Take them at different times of day or on different days, and the readings may vary greatly.

The important reasons? In part, fluctuating physiology, but also measurement errors, the limits of measurement accuracy, and observer variation. Examining the same patient, no two doctors will report exactly the same results, and the results may be grossly different. If six doctors examine a patient with a faint heart murmer, only one or two may have the skill or keen hearing to detect it. Experimental results so typically differ from one time to the next that scientific and medical fakers — a Boston cancer researcher, for example — have been detected by the unusual regularity of their reported results, with numbers agreeing too well and the same results appearing time after time, with not enough variation from patient to patient.

Biological variation is the most important cause of variation in physiology and medicine. Different patients, and the same patients, react differently to the same treatment. Disease rates differ in different parts of the country and among different populations, and — alas, nothing is simple — there is natural variation within the same population.

Every population, after all, is a collection of individuals, each with many characteristics. Each characteristic, or *variable,* such as height, has a *distribution* of values from person to person, and — if we would know something about the whole population — we must have some handy summaries of the distribution. We can't get much out of a list of 10,000 measurements, so we need single values that summarize many measurements.

Enter here the familiar *average* or, more exactly, the *mean, median,* and *mode.* These and a few other measures can give us some idea of the look of the whole and its many measurable properties, or *parameters.*

When most of us speak of an average, we mean simply the *mean* or *arithmetic average,* the sum of all the values divided by the number of values. The mean is no mean tool; it is a good way to get a typical number, but it has limitations, especially when there are some extreme values. There is said to be a memorial in a Siberian town to a fictitious Count Smerdlovski, the world's champion at Russian roulette. On the average he won, but his actual record was 73 and 1.[21]

If you look at the average salary in a hospital, you will not know that half the personnel may be working for the minimum wage, while a few hundred persons make $100,000 or more a year. You may learn more here from the *median,* the figure that divides a population into two equal halves. The median can be of value when a group has a few members with extreme values, like the 400-pounder at an obesity clinic whose other patients weigh from 180 to 200 pounds. If he leaves, the patients' mean weight might drop by 10 pounds, but the median might drop just 1 pound.[22]

The most frequently occurring number or value in a distribution is called the *mode.* When the median and the mode are about the same, or even more when mean, median, and mode are roughly equal, you can feel comfortable about knowing the typical value.

You still need to know something about the exceptions, in short, the *dispersion* (or spread or scatter) of the entire distribution. One measure of spread is the *range.* It tells you the lowest and highest values. It might inform you, for example, that the salaries in that hospital range from $10,000 to $250,000.

You can also divide your values into 100 *percentiles,* so you can say someone or something falls into the 10th or 71st percentile, or into *quartiles* (fourths) or *quintiles* (fifths). One useful measure is the *interquartile range,* the interval between the 75th and 25th percentiles—this is the distribution in the middle, which avoids the extreme values at each end. Or you can divide a distribution into *subgroups*—those with incomes from $10,000 to $20,000, for example, or ages 20 to 29, 30 to 39, and so on.

All these values can easily be plotted. With many of the things that scientists, economists, or others measure—IQs, for example, and other test scores—we typically tend to see a familiar, bell-shaped *normal distribution,* high in the middle, low at each end, or *tail.* This is the classic *Gaussian curve,* named after the 19th-century German mathematician Karl Friedrich Gauss. But you may also find that the plot has two or more peaks or clusters, a *bimodal* or *multimodal distribution.*

A widely used number, the *standard deviation,* can reveal a great deal. No matter how it sounds, it is not the average distance from the mean but a more complex figure.* Unlike the range, this handy figure takes full account of every value to tell how spread out things are—how dispersed the measurements. In what one statistician calls a truly remarkable generalization, in most sets of measurement "and without regard to what is being measured" only 1 measurement in 3 will deviate from the average by more than 1 standard deviation, only 1 in 20 by more than 2 standard deviations, and only 1 in 100 by more than 2.57 standard deviations.

"Once you know the standard deviation in a normal, bell-shaped distribution," according to Thomas Louis, "you can draw the whole picture of the data. You can visualize the shape of the curve without even drawing the picture, since the larger the variation of the numbers, the larger the standard deviation and the more spread out the curve—and vice versa."

---

*There is more than one way to calculate it, and there are several variations, depending on the statistician's purpose. A common one is to add the squares of the differences between each number and the mean, then divide that number by the total number of squares, often referred to as the *variance* (minus 1 if you're looking at a sample of a population rather than the whole population). Then calculate the square root of the result. As in

$$s = \sqrt{\frac{\Sigma(X - \overline{X})^2}{n - 1}}$$

Sometimes statisticians calculate the *standard deviation of the mean*—this because the mean, being an average, is less variable than single measurements. Some call this the *standard error* or *standard error of the mean.* As in

$$s_{\overline{x}} = \frac{s}{\sqrt{n}}$$

All the above are measures of dispersion.

Example: If the average score of all students who take the SAT college entrance test is relatively low and the spread—the standard deviation—relatively large, this creates a very long-tailed, low-humped curve of test scores, ranging, say, from around 300 to 1500. But if the average score of a group of brighter students entering an elite college is high, the standard deviation of the scores will be less and the curve will be high-humped and short-tailed, going from maybe 900 to 1500.

"If I just told you the means of two such distributions, you might say they were the same," another scientist says. "But if I reported the means and the standard deviations, you'd know they were different, with a lot more variations in one."

From a human standpoint, variation tells us that it takes more than averages to describe individuals. Biologist Stephen Jay Gould learned in 1982 that he had a serious form of cancer. The literature told him the median survival was only eight months after discovery. Three years later he wrote in *Discover*, "All evolutionary biologists know that means and medians are the abstractions," while variation is "the reality," meaning "half the people will live longer" than eight months.

Since he was young, since his disease had been diagnosed early, and since he would receive the best possible treatment, he decided he had a good chance of being at the far end of the curve. He calculated that the curve must be skewed well to the right, as the left half of the distribution had to be "scrunched up between zero and eight months, but the upper right half [could] extend out for years." He concluded, "I saw no reason why I shouldn't be in that small tail. . . . I would have time to think, to plan and to fight." Also, since he was being placed on an experimental new treatment, he might if fortune smiled "be in the first cohort of a new distribution with . . . a right tail extending to death by natural causes at advanced old age."[23]

Statistics cannot tell us whether fortune will smile, only that such reasoning is sound.

Studies, Good and Bad

4

Why think? Why not try an experiment?

—John Hunter
18th-century British anatomist

Sit down before fact as a little child, be prepared to give up every preconceived notion, follow humbly wherever and to whatever abysses nature leads, or you shall learn nothing.

—Thomas Henry Huxley

This is the part I always hate.

—A mathematician as he approaches the equal sign (in a Sidney Harris cartoon in *American Scientist*)

THERE is no disease that strikes older people more tragically than Alzheimer's disease, which makes a useless tangle of the brain. At a prestigious New England university a research team imaginatively inserted catheters into the skulls of four patients aged 64 to 73 to deliver a continuous infusion of either a theoretically promising drug or, alternately, an ineffectual saline solution for comparison.

After 18 months the investigators published a paper saying that according to observations by the patients' families, three patients showed marked improvement and the fourth at least held his own. Fascinating, of course. Some reporters learned of the work and began inquiring. The investigators let a TV crew do a story and also held a news conference, with one patient brought forth for on-camera testimonials. Except for some newspapers that decided to print nothing, the story flew far and wide.

The head investigator, a chief resident in neurosurgery, cautioned that the results, though encouraging, were "very early" and "certainly do not prove this is an effective treatment." He advised healthy skepticism. But headlines unequivocally read: "Alzheimer's Test Found Successful," "Alzheimer's: A New Promise," "First Breakthrough Against Alzheimer's," "Pump Offers Hope," "Possible Alzheimer's Cure."

Within two months the medical center logged 2,600 phone calls, mainly from desperate families, and critics began asking why a press conference had been held, since a study of only four patients — with unblinded investigators getting their assessments from hopeful families — meant little.

Harvard's Dr. Jay Winsten concluded that "the decision to hold a press conference . . . far outweighed in impact the modulating effect of the investigators' qualifying language. The visual impact of [one] patient's on-camera testimonials all but guaranteed that TV coverage would oversell the research, despite any qualifying language."[1]

When dubious claims are made — about Alzheimer's, a new cancer drug, a possible AIDS cure — and the claims get widely reported, there is commonly a lot of postmortem clucking and soul-searching among reporters and editors. Then someone else makes some sensational claim, and the same thing may happen all over again.

The biggest error in medical science, according to Dr. Thomas Chalmers, is "the uncontrolled pilot study in which the investigators try a treatment on 10 patients, and if it seems to work . . . are tempted to report it" to fellow scientists, let alone the media.[2]

All science is only a stab at the truth. Even with the best of statistics, "We scientists don't know how to tell the whole truth," Mosteller reminds us.[3] Outside this honest limitation lie vast realms of inadequate science with plausible-sounding yet shaky statistics. A French physician, Pierre Charles Alexandre Louis, said 150 years ago, "The only reproach which can be made to the numerical method" is that it "requires much more labor and time than the most distinguished members of our profession" often give it. "Some days," says one modern statistician, "I think every idiot in the country who can put his hands on a computer program thinks he's a statistician."

The big problems of statistics, say its best practitioners, have little to do with computations and formulas. They have to do with judgment, we're told, with how to design a study, how to conduct it, then analyze and interpret the results. In a day of frenzied media competition for the public's eye and ear—and many chances to do harm by shaky reporting—journalism too calls for sophisticated judgment. How, then, can we have some hope of telling which studies seem credible, which we should report?

A fundamental principle is that every conscientiously conducted study has a careful *design:* a method or plan of attack to include the right kind and number of patients or petri dishes and to try to eliminate bias. Different problems require different methods, and one of the most basic questions in science is, *Can this kind of experiment, this design, yield the answer?*

This is not a simple question for a reporter to answer, but there is much we can know. What kinds of studies, what kinds of numbers and controls and methods, should we look for?

Experiments versus Seductive Anecdotes

Students and eggs can be graded, citizens and cities can be credit-rated, and scientific evidence can be weighed according to what has been called a hierarchy of evidence. Some kinds of studies carry little weight, some more, some a great deal.

Science and medicine started with *anecdotes,* unreliable as far as generalization is concerned, yet provocative. Anecdotes matured into systematic *observation,* the most ancient form of science. Observation told the ancients much about the stars, it told the pharaohs' physicians much about the sick, and it is still important, for simple "eyeballing" has developed into *data collection* and the recording of *case histories*. These are respectable, yea, indispensable methods yet still only one part of science. Case histories may not be typical, or they may reflect the beholder. Medicine continues to be plagued by Big Authorities who insist, "I know what I see."

There can be useful, even inspired, observation and analysis of *natural experiments*. Excess fluoride in some waters hardened teeth, and this observation led to fluoridation of drinking water to prevent tooth decay. There are also man's inadvertent experiments, disastrous and benign, to be studied. Hiroshima triggered wide analysis of the effects of nuclear radiation, invaluable yet frustrating because there were no good measures of exposure levels, a gap that has caused confusion and controversy ever since.

In 1585 or so, Galileo dropped those weights from a tower and helped invent the *scientific experiment:* a study in which the experimenter *controls* the conditions — controlled conditions are the heart of the experimental method — and records the effect. Experiments on objects, animals, germs, and people matured into the modern *experimental study,* in which the experimenter typically changes only one or some other planned number of variables to see the outcome.

Clinical Trials

The experimental method is the essence of experimental medicine's current "gold standard":[4] the *controlled, randomized clinical trial.* At its best, the investigator tests a treatment or drug or some other intervention by randomly selecting at least two comparable groups, the *experimental group* that is tested or treated and a *control group* that is observed for comparison.

True clinical trials are expensive and difficult. It has been estimated that of 100 scheduled trials, 60 are abandoned, not implemented, or not completed, whether for lack of funds, difficulty in recruiting or keeping patients, toxicity or other problems, or, sometimes, rapid evidence of a difference in effect (making continued denial of effective treatment to a control group unethical). Another 20 trials produce no noteworthy results, and just 20, results worth publishing. Clinical trials nonetheless are called the strongest, most precise, most decisive way to evaluate medical interventions and learn true causation. Randomized clinical trials proved that new drugs could cut the heart attack death rate, that treating hypertension could prevent strokes, and that polio, measles, and hepatitis vaccines worked. No doctor, observing a limited number of patients, could have shown these things.

Types of clinical studies include the following:

• Among the most reliable are *parallel studies* comparing similar groups given different treatments, or a treatment versus no treatment. But such studies are not always possible.

• In *crossover studies* the same patients get two or more treatments in succession and act as their own controls. Similarly, *self-controlled studies* evaluate an experimental treatment by control observations during periods of no treatment or of some standard treatment. There are pitfalls here. Treatment A might affect the outcome of treatment B, despite the usual use of a *washout period* between study periods. Patients become acclimated: They may become more tolerant of pain or side effects or, now more health-conscious, may change their ways. The controls—the patients in a control group—don't always behave in parallel studies either: In one large-scale trial of methods to lower blood cholesterol and risk of heart disease, many controls adopted some of the same methods—quitting cigarette smoking, eating fewer fats—and reduced their risk too.

• Investigators often use *historical controls* (meaning comparison with old records: historically the cure rate has been 30 percent, say, and the new therapy cures 60 percent) or other *external controls* (such as comparison with other studies). These controls are often misleading—the groups compared are frequently not comparable, the treatments may have been given by different methods—but they are still at times useful.

What Makes a Study Honest?

Obviously, all studies, including the best, have potential pitfalls:

• *Lack of adequate controls* is fatal if you really want to put the results in the bank.

• The *group or sample studied,* 10 people or 10,000, must be *large* enough to get a valid result and *representative* enough to apply to a larger population. Because people vary so widely in their reactions, and a few patients can fool you, fair-sized groups of patients are usually needed. And enough of the right kind of subjects are needed for a suitable sample. Picking patients for a medical study is no different from picking citizens to be questioned in a political poll. In both, a sample is studied, and *inferences*—the outcome of an election, the results in patients in general—are made for a larger population.

To get a large enough sample, medical researchers more and more try to conduct *multicenter trials,* which are appealing because they can include hundreds of patients, but expensive and tricky because one must try to maintain similar patient selection and quality control at 10 or 100 institutions. Successful multicenter trials established the value of controlling hypertension to prevent strokes. They demonstrated the strong probability that less extensive surgery is as effective as more drastic surgery for many breast cancers.

• The *sample should be randomized*—divided by some random method into comparable experimental and control groups. Randomization can easily be violated. A doctor assigning patients to treatment A or B may, seeing a particular type of patient, say or think, "This patient will be better on B."

If treatment B has been established as better than A, there should be no random study in the first place and certainly no study of that doctor's patient. When randomization is violated, "the trial's guarantee of lack of bias goes down the drain," says one critique. As a result, patients who consent to randomization are often assigned to study groups according to a list of computer-generated random numbers.

• *To combat bias* — the influence of confounding variables — and get answers applicable to various populations, the sample or study population must often be *stratified,* or separated into groups by age, sex, socioeconomic status, and so on. Failure to stratify can hide true associations. The role of high-absorbency tampons in toxic shock syndrome was clarified only when the cases were broken down by precise type of tampon used.

The identification of important subcategories of patients can be tricky indeed. A study of open-heart surgery patients may fail to separate out those who had to wait for their surgery. But some patients die waiting, and those left are relatively stronger patients who do better, on the average, than those treated immediately after diagnosis.

We reporters may also fail to pay attention to stratification, or distribution. In early 1985 the President's Council of Economic Advisers reported that — to quote the page-one lead in a major newspaper — "elderly Americans have achieved economic parity with the rest of the population and no longer are a disadvantaged group." Not for several paragraphs, now on an inside page, did the story note that "there's a lot of variability," and older people are also "more likely . . . to have members with incomes below the average of their age group."[5] In short, there are still many elderly trapped in poverty.

• *To combat bias in investigators or patients,* studies should be *blinded* — to the extent feasible, *single-, double-,* or, best of all, *triple-blinded,* so that neither the doctors nor the nurses administering a treatment nor the patients nor those who assess the results know whether today's pill is treatment A, treatment B, or an ineffective *placebo.* Otherwise, a doctor or patient who yearns for a good result may see or feel one when the "right" drug is given. There is a tale of an overzealous receptionist who, knowing which patients were getting the real drug and not the placebo, was so encouraging to these patients that they began saying they felt good, willy-nilly.[6]

Barring observant receptionists, the use of a placebo — from the Latin meaning "I shall please" — may help maintain blindness. Placebos actually give some relief in a third of all patients, on the average, in various conditions. The effect is usually temporary, however, and a truly effective drug ought to work substantially better than the placebo.

Blinding is often impossible or unwise. Some treatments don't lend themselves to it, and some drugs quickly reveal themselves by various effects. But an unblinded test is a weaker test.

• Finally, what makes a study honest is honesty. John Bailar warns of deliberate or careless deceptions that seem to be universally accepted today, practices that sometimes have much value but at other times are "inappropriate and improper and, to the extent that they are deceptive, unethical." Among them: the selective reporting of findings, leaving out some that might not fit the conclusion; the reporting of a single study in multiple fragments, when the whole might not sound so good; and the failure to report the low power of some studies, their inability to detect a result even if one existed.[7]

Dr. Charles Moertel of the Mayo Clinic says,

> Probably the majority of cancer patients treated with chemotherapy today are receiving regimens that have not been proved effective by randomized trial. . . . Many articles published in our major journals make claims for fantastic therapeutic accomplishments with no randomized controls. . . . Many, if not most, of the randomized studies . . . are of such poor quality that their results are unbelievable. . . . Precious few have withstood the scrutiny of carefully designed confirmatory scientific study.

He calls a multitude of poor methods statistical legerdemain: "the games we play, trying to squeeze out that little bit of breakthrough." Why the pressure to play them? "Salvation," Dr.

David Salsburg answers. "Fruit in this world (increases in salary, prestige, invitations to speak) and beyond this life (continual references in the citation index)."[8]

Epidemiology: Hippocrates to AIDS

Clinical studies deal with patients. Epidemiology deals with populations, which sometimes are large groups of patients. Epidemiology seeks the causes of both health and disease by placing a population under its own kind of microscope, the *epidemiological investigation*.

Epidemiological studies in many ways parallel clinical studies — some studies are both — and are subject to many of the same pitfalls and rules, like avoiding bias and stratifying to get the right answers about the right subgroups. An old saw, in fact, goes, an epidemiologist is a physician broken down by age and sex.

Epidemiology in its early days was concerned wholly with epidemics of typhoid, smallpox, and other infections. But epidemiologists today also ask, "What should we eat and how should we live to stay healthy?" and they study large groups to see how the healthiest and unhealthiest live. Hippocrates has been called the first environmentalist because he observed that it was healthier to live in high places than in low ones. Anticipating today's environmentalists, he blamed bad air and bad water and may have been partly right. But he failed to stratify; otherwise he might have noticed that the people who lived high were also wealthier and better nourished than those who lived low.[9]

In 1740 Percival Pott scored a famous epidemiological success by observing the high rate of scrotum cancer in London's chimney sweeps and correctly blaming it on their exposure to soot — burned organic material, much like a smoked cigarette. A century later, John Snow, plotting London cholera cases on a map and noting a cluster around one source of drinking water, removed the handle from the now famed Broad Street pump and helped end a deadly epidemic. The 19th-century French advocate of statistical methods, Pierre Louis, observed hospital patients and helped stop the use of bleeding as a treatment. Ignaz Semmelweis showed that doctors' dirty hands transmitted deadly childbed fever to mothers.

Modern epidemiologists successfully indicted smoking as a cause of lung cancer and heart disease and identified the association of fats and cholesterol with clogging of the arteries. They evaluate vaccines, assess new methods of health care delivery, and track down the causes of new scourges like AIDS, toxic shock syndrome, and Legionnaires' disease, all by several methods. All are valuable. All are full of traps.

• Epidemiology, like all of science, started with *observational* studies, and these remain important. They are weak and uncertain, we have noted, when it comes to determining cause and effect. Yet observation is how we first learned of the unfortunate effects of toxic rain, Agent Orange, cigarette smoking, and many sometimes helpful, sometimes harmful medications—and of certain sexual practices and addicts' use of dirty needles on AIDS.

• Some observational studies are simply *descriptive*—describing the incidence, prevalence, and mortality rates of various diseases, for example. Other, *analytic* studies seek to analyze or explain: the Seven-Country Study, for example, that helped associate high meat and dairy fat and cholesterol consumption with excess risk of coronary heart disease. *Ecological* studies look for links between environmental conditions and illness. Human migrations—like that of the Japanese who come to the United States, eat more fat, and get more disease than they did in Japan—are among valuable *natural experiments*.

• The simplest observational measurement is a *count*. *Sampling* is just a more sophisticated kind of count. You can't count or question everybody, so you seek a sample that represents the whole. Many epidemiological *surveys* rely on samples—among them, government surveys of health and nutritional habits. Samples and surveys often use *questionnaires* to get information.

A sample or survey is never more than a snapshot of the

scene at the moment; it can't portray an ever-changing picture unless frequently repeated. Questionnaires may be no better than the quality of the answers, written or verbal. One survey compared patients' reporting of their current chronic illnesses with those their doctors recorded. The patients failed to mention almost half of the conditions the doctors detected over the course of a year. And whether it comes to illness, diets, or drinking, people tend to put themselves in the best possible light. They often say both yes and no to the same question in different form. A survey may stand or fall on the use of sophisticated ways to get accurate information.

• Epidemiologists' studies may also be *prevalence studies, case-control studies,* or *cohort studies.* A *prevalence study,* also called a *current* or *cross-sectional study* is a wide-angle snapshot of a population: a look at the rate of disease X or at toxic agent X and its possible effects by age, sex, or other variables. A political poll is such a study: A cross section of the nation is examined in a period of a few days.

A *case-control study* examines *cases* and *controls* for a close-up of a disease's relationship to other factors in a small, intensively examined group. The nation hears of cases of toxic shock syndrome, mainly in young women. The federal Centers for Disease Control launches a *field investigation* to find a series of patients, or *cases,* confirm the diagnosis, then interview them and their families and other contacts to assemble careful case histories that cover, hopefully, all possible causes or associations. This group is then compared with a randomly selected but matched *compeer group,* or *control group,* of healthy young women of like age and other characteristics.

The results need to be interpreted with great caution, but the case-control study is often a quick, highly useful and relatively easy, low-cost first approach or fishing expedition to assemble clues about causes or even a working hypothesis. Or it may test some hypothesis. A case-control study pinpointed the use of tampons (later found to be certain high-absorbency ones) as the main villain in toxic shock. The relationship of cigarette

smoking to lung cancer, the association of birth control pills with
blood vessel problems, and the transmission patterns of AIDS
were identified in case-control studies that pointed to the need
for broader investigation.

Cohort or *incidence studies* are motion pictures. They pick a
group of people, or *cohort*—a cohort was a unit of a Roman
legion—often stratify or divide them into subgroups, then follow
them over time, often for years, to see how some disease or
diseases develop. These studies are costly and difficult. Subjects
drop out or disappear. Large numbers must be studied to see
rare events. But cohort studies can be powerful instruments and
substitutes for randomized experiments that would be ethically
impossible. You can't ethically expose a group to an agent that
you suspect would cause a disease. You can watch a group so
exposed.

The noted Framingham study of ways of life that might be
associated with developing heart disease has followed more than
5,000 residents of that Massachusetts town since 1948. The
American Cancer Society's 1952–55 study of 187,783 men aged
50 to 69, with 11,780 of them dying during that period, did
much to establish that cigarette smoking was strongly associated
with developing lung cancer.[10]

• Many epidemiological, as well as clinical, studies are
handicapped because they must be *retrospective*. They look back
in time—at medical records, vital statistics, or people's recollec-
tions (for example, those collected in interviews in a case-control
study). People who have a disease are questioned to try to find
common habits or exposures. Women with cervical cancer are
interviewed to see how many took possibly guilty hormones and
how many did not. People who live around a Love Canal are
asked if they have been ill.

Retrospective studies are notoriously unreliable. Memories
fail or play tricks. Old records are poor and misleading. Definitions of diseases and methods of diagnosis vary sharply over the
years. The patients you find may not be representative. A retrospective study, however intriguing, generally only says that
there may be something here that ought to be investigated.

(There are exceptions. Dr. Gary Friedman writes, "A retrospective study can be quite reliable if based on data carefully collected in the past. A revealing study of mortality in radiologists was a retrospective cohort study based on good data.")

• A *prospective study,* in contrast—like the Framingham and the American Cancer Society studies—looks forward. It focuses sharply on a selected group who are all followed by the same statistical and medical techniques. Dr. Eugene Robin at Stanford tells how four separate retrospective clinical studies affirmed the accuracy of a test for blood clots in the lungs. When an adequate prospective clinical trial was done, most of the backward looks were proved wrong.[11]

• Epidemiology also includes *experimental studies,* the classical experiments of science on a larger human scale. These are typically *intervention studies.* There is some intervention or manipulation; something is done to some of the subjects.

The massive and hugely successful 1954 field trial of the Salk polio vaccine was a classic intervention trial and a clinical trial too, with 401,974 first- to third-graders assigned at random to either a vaccinated group or a control group injected with a placebo, or dummy shot—and another 947,171 children divided between vaccinated second-graders and unvaccinated first- and third-graders acting as controls. In addition, in all participating states or counties, the investigators studied and counted all cases of polio in a grand total of 1,829,916 children: those who had taken part in the study and those who had not. In the placebo areas, the study was also triple-blinded: neither the vaccinators, the subjects, nor the doctors who examined the subjects later for polio knew which children got which kind of shot.[12]

Another successful intervention study, a *community trial,* established the value of fluoridating water supplies to prevent tooth decay. Some towns had their water fluoridated; some did not. Blinding was impossible, but the striking difference in dental caries that resulted could not have been caused by any placebo effect.

Questions Reporters Can Ask 5

Just because Dr. Famous or Dr. Bigshot says this is what he found doesn't mean it is necessarily so.

— Dr. Arnold Relman

Ask to see the numbers, not just the pretty colors.

— Dr. Richard Margolin
National Institutes of Health,
describing PET scans to reporters

WHAT questions should we reporters ask—to make our news solid, to report the more valid claims and ignore the weak and phony? When a scientist or physician or anyone else says, "I've discovered that . . . ," what should we ask?

In 1949, a year after Britain's National Health Service— "socialized medicine"—was launched, my editors sent me to Britain to see how it was working. A bit stumped, I asked Dr. Morris Fishbein, the provocative genius who long edited the *Journal of the American Medical Association,* "How can I, a reporter, tell whether a doctor is doing a good job?" He immediately said, "Ask him how often he has a patient take off his shirt."

His lesson was plain: No physical examination is complete unless the patient takes off his or her clothes. Most reporters are not skilled statisticians, but we can ask some similarly revealing questions. Many of these are not even statistical, just simple ones that, like Fishbein's, probe soft spots and often disclose either a conscientious approach or one that can't be trusted.

We can learn here from one method of science. We said

earlier that a properly skeptical scientist, starting a study and seeking truth, often begins with a *null hypothesis* — that treatment A is no better than treatment B, that there's nothing there — then sees whether or not the evidence disproves it. This approach is much like the law's presumption of innocence: It is for the prosecutor to prove beyond reasonable doubt that the suspect is guilty. A reporter, without being cynical and believing nothing, should be equally skeptical and greet every claim by saying, in words or thought, "Show me."

If an investigator or claimant is competent and has a good case, you may have to ask none or very few of these questions, since a good scientific presentation should answer most of them for you. The need for a lot of questions could itself tell you something.

Here are some possible questions, then, some of them simple and obvious ones, a few more technical for those who might want to ask them.

How do you know? Have you done a study? Was there an experiment? What is the evidence? Or is the approach just anecdotal? Answers like "In my experience . . . ," "In my hands . . . ," "I've seen 20 cases . . . ," and "There are four cases in our block . . . " may be interesting, may be worth scientific investigation, may be worth a cautious news story, but there is not yet anything like certainty.

What kind of study was it? Was there a systematic research plan or design? And a protocol or set of rules?

What was the study design or method: observational, experimental, case-control, prospective, retrospective, or what? (See the previous chapter for kinds of studies and their uses and limits.) "A lot of people just scrounge around and try to come up with some conclusion without any real plan or design at the start," one medical editor reports. *Was the design drawn before you started your study? What specific questions or hypotheses did you set out to test or answer?*

Why did you do it that way? Do you think it was the right kind of study to get the answer to this question or problem?

Was it a true human experiment, if possible, with comparable groups picked at random for comparison? If not, why not? And what was the substitute?

If an investigator patiently — you hope — tells you about an acceptable-sounding design, that's worth a brownie point. If the answer is "Huh?" or a nasty one, that may tell you something else.

Are you presenting preliminary data or something fairly conclusive? Are you presenting a conclusion or a hypothesis for further study? "Preliminary" and "interesting" can mean "unproved."

If the result is not reasonably conclusive, should there be further studies and what kind?

How many subjects, patients, cases, or people are you talking about? Are these numbers large enough, statistically rigorous enough, to get the answers you want? Was there an adequate number of patients to show a difference between treatments? Why are you calling a press conference to report on four patients?

Small numbers can sometimes carry weight. And they may sometimes be the only ones possible. "Sometimes small samples are the best we can do," one researcher says. But larger numbers are always more likely to pass statistical muster.

The number studied can also depend on the subject. A thorough physiological study of five cases of some difficult disorder may be important. One new case of smallpox would be a shocker in a world in which smallpox has supposedly been eliminated. In June 1981 the federal Centers for Disease Control reported that five young men, all active homosexuals, had been treated for *Pneumocystis carinii* pneumonia at three Los Angeles hospitals.[1] This alerted the world to what soon became the AIDS epidemic.

Who were your subjects? How were they selected? What were your criteria for admission to the study? Were rigorous laboratory tests used to define the patients, or were clinical diagnoses (necessarily less reliable) used?

Was the assignment of subjects to treatment or other intervention randomized? Randomization should give every patient a 50 percent chance of being assigned to one group or the other of a two-armed study (one comparing two groups). *Were the patients admitted to the study before the randomization?* This helps eliminate bias. *How was the randomization done?*

If the subjects weren't randomized, why not? One statistician says, "If it is a nonrandomized study, a biased investigator can get some extraordinary results by carefully picking his subjects."

Was there a control or comparison group? If not, the study will always be weaker. *Who or what were your controls or bases for comparison?* In other words: *When you say you have such and such a result, what are you comparing it with? Are the study or patient group and the control group similar in all respects but the treatment or other variable being studied?*

Vogt calls "comparison of non-comparable groups probably . . . the single most common error in the medical and popular literature on health and disease."[2]

Do you have reason to believe your subjects and controls were representative of the general population? Or the particular population — those with the disease or condition you are interested in? The answers here go a long way toward answering these questions: *To what populations are the results applicable? Would the association hold for other groups?*

If your groups are not comparable to the general population or some important populations, have you taken steps to adjust for this? Either statistical adjustment or stratification of your sample to find out about specific groups, or both? Samples can be adjusted for age, for example, to make an older- or younger-than-average sample more nearly comparable to the general populace. (More on applicability and stratification after a bit.)

Was the study blind? In a study comparing drugs or other forms of treatment with a placebo or dummy treatment, did (1) those administering the treatment, (2) those getting it, and (3) those assessing the outcome know who was getting what, or were they indeed blinded, knowing only that they were comparing A and B (or A, B, and C, perhaps)?

Could those giving or getting the treatment have easily guessed which was which by a difference in reaction or taste or other results?

Not every study can be a blind study. One researcher says, "There can be ethical problems in not telling patients what drug they're taking and the possible side effects. People are not guinea pigs." True enough, but a blinded study will always carry more conviction.

Were there other accepted quality controls? For example, making sure (perhaps by counting pills or studying urine samples) that the patients supposed to take a pill really took it.

Were you able to follow your protocol or study plan?

If there were questionnaires, interviews, or a survey: *Were the questions likely to elicit accurate, reliable answers? Was it really possible to get accurate answers to these questions?*

Sampling is as common in medical studies as in political polling. Every study examines a sample, not the whole population. The sample must be reasonably accurate to give valid results. But badly worded questions can also distort the results. Respondents' answers can differ sharply, depending on how questions are asked. Example: In one study 1,153 subjects were asked which is safer, a treatment that kills 10 percent of every 100 patients or a treatment with a 90 percent survival rate? More people voted for the second way of saying precisely the same thing.[3]

People commonly give inaccurate answers to sensitive questions, such as those about sexual behavior. They are notoriously inaccurate in reporting their own medical histories, even those of recent months.

Ask: *Did you pretest your questions for effectiveness before doing your actual survey?*

Also: *What was your nonresponse rate? Do you report it?*

In any study: *How many of your study subjects completed the course? Do you account for those who dropped out and tell why they did?*

Every study has dropouts. McMaster University's Dr. David Sackett says, "Patients do not disappear . . . for trivial reasons. Rather, they leave . . . because they refuse therapy, recover, die, or retire to the Sunbelt with their permanent disability." If an investigator ignores those who didn't do well and dropped out, it can make the outcome look better. If those who died of "other causes" are listed among "survivors" of the disease being investigated—this is sometimes done on the theory that, after all, they didn't die of the target cause—it can make a treatment look better unless there are equal numbers of such deaths in every branch of the study.

Sackett adds, "The loss to follow-up of 10 per cent of the original inception cohort is cause for concern. If 20 per cent or more are not accounted for, the results . . . are probably not worth reading."[4] (On which Dr. Thomas Vogt comments, "Generally true, but utterly dependent on the situation.")

Professor Warren Burkett of the University of Texas adds a few related and pointed questions: *"Does the paper or publication contain all results of all experiments?* Support for a hypothesis has sometimes been made to seem stronger by selective reporting . . . including only the data that most closely fit the theory. *To what extent has the data offered . . . been smoothed from the raw data?* . . . It is not unknown for researchers to clip and round data to make them fit [their] predicted results" (italics mine).[5]

How long was the study's follow-up? How long do patients ordinarily survive with this disease? Were your patients followed long enough to really know the outcomes, good or bad?

And: *How thorough was the follow-up?* In one report on amebiasis—a disease caused by an amoeba—the diagnosis was made by finding the amoeba in one of three consecutive stools, but a cure was declared after observing just one negative stool. "It does pay to read with care," a medical professor observes.

Could your results have occurred just by chance? Have any statistical tests been applied to test this?

Did you calculate a P value? Was it favorable—.05 or less? (Reported as < .05; see Chapter 3.) *P* values and confidence statements need not be regarded as straitjackets, but like jury verdicts, they indicate reasonable doubt or reasonable certainty.

Remember that positive findings are more likely to be reported and published than negative findings. Remember that a favorable-sounding *P* value of < .05 means only that there is just 1 chance in 20, or a 5 percent probability, that the statistics could have come out this way by pure chance *when there was actually no effect*—so 1 in every 20 statistically significant results may be a misleading false positive.

There are also ways and ways of arriving at *P* values. For example, an investigator may choose to report one of several *end points:* death, length of survival, blood pressure, other measurements, or just the patient's condition on leaving the hospital. All can be important, but a *P* value can be misleading if the wrong one is picked or emphasized.

You might want to ask: *Are all the important end points and their* P *values reported?* Also: *Was the test giving the* P *value the appropriate test, as planned in your written protocol, or did you finally do more than one kind of test?* (And perhaps report only the best answer?) *What were the other values?*

Did you collaborate with a statistician in both your design and your analysis? A statistician's collaboration often may be indicated in a credit or footnote.

In studies seeking *cause and effect,* remember that association is not necessarily causation. Rutgers' Dr. Michael Greenberg reminds us, "Mathematical methods cannot establish proof of cause and effect. They can indicate the probability that a relationship occurred by chance, can sometimes quantify the existing relationship between actions and effects, and can under the best circumstances be used to predict the impact of actions even

if the complex phenomena driving them are not understood.
. . . View mathematical associations with a healthy degree of
skepticism."

A true experiment, controlling all variables, can sometimes
prove cause and effect almost surely. This is easier in physics
and chemistry than in human biology. When, then, does a close
association in an observational study (rather than a controlled
experiment) indicate causation? There are several possible criteria that you can ask about:

Is the association consistent? Are similar results usually found in
different places and by different research methods?

How strong is the association? If risk is an appropriate way of
describing a particular situation: *What is the relative risk, or the risk
ratio?* The word "strong" is used here in its mathematical sense.
It mainly means the *magnitude* of an effect or risk, the *odds* favor-
ing the *outcome of interest* versus no such outcome.

A *relative risk,* or *risk ratio,* compares two rates by dividing
one by the other. In an American Cancer Society smoking study
(see page 46) the lung cancer mortality rate in nonsmokers aged
55 to 69 was 19 per 100,000 per year; the risk in smokers was
188 per 100,000. Since 188 divided by 19 equals 9.89, the
smokers were about 9.9 times more likely to die from lung
cancer—their relative risk was 9.9.[6] That's strong!

Is there an impressive dose-response, or cause-and-effect, curve—a
curve or *gradient* that shows that the greater the exposure to the
agent, or cause, the greater the effect? Heavy smokers are indeed at greater risk than moderate smokers, and moderate
smokers at greater risk than light smokers. (In some cases—this
is an unsettled matter—there may be a threshold effect, an effect
only after some minimum dose.)

Another way of asking about risk and response: *What is the
correlation coefficient*—the extent to which a set of measurements of
the association is *linear?* A perfect linear relationship, or correlation, between two observations or variables would show up as a
straight, steadily rising set of *data points*—in everyday language,
a straight line on a graph. A perfect positive correlation or,

linear relationship, is given the value +1; +.5 would be a lesser but still interesting relationship; −1 or any negative figure indicates an *inverse* or *negative relationship,* such as a runner's speed going down as his weight goes up. A correlation of zero means no consistent association.

How specific is the association? Does a supposed cause lead to many supposed effects? Or does an effect depend on many supposed causes? Such associations are less specific, and thus more suspect, until positive evidence piles up. Smoking indeed causes many effects. A lung disease, asbestosis, is most common when there is exposure to both asbestos and cigarette smoke.

Does the supposed cause precede the effect? Is a supposed biological association epidemiologically plausible? One strong argument for a cause-and-effect relationship between high consumption of saturated fats and cholesterol and coronary heart disease is that populations on such diets generally develop more such disease than those on leaner diets.

Does the association make biological sense? Does it agree with current biological and physiological knowledge? You can't follow this test out the window. Much biological fact is ill understood. Also, Mosteller warns, "*Someone* nearly always will claim to see a [biological or physiological] association. But the people who know the most may not be willing to."[7]

Finally, look for the real why. Ask: *Are there other possible explanations? Did you look for other explanations — confounders, or confounding variables,* that may be producing or helping produce the association? Sometimes we read that married people live longer than singles. Does marriage really increase life span, or may medical or other problems make some people less likely to marry and also die sooner? Maybe the Dutch thought storks brought babies because better-off families had more chimneys, more storks, and more babies.

Did you take steps to control or adjust for other possible explanations? Did you do a stratified analysis — a breakdown of the data by strata like sex, race, socioeconomic status, geographical area, occupation? Men commonly have more bronchitis and cirrhosis of the liver than women because they drink more. They also have more heart disease, possibly because they've smoked longer, possibly because some hormones protect women. Only stratified analyses will bring out such differences.

Did you do an analysis (a regression or some other form of multivariate analysis) to try to identify the important variable or variables? Such analyses can often reveal the strongest associations. They can also be misused, and they are not always needed or appropriate. Some sophisticated questions, when appropriate: *How many such analyses did you have to run to decide on the appropriate one?* Sometimes the more analyses, the worse the study. *How many variables did you consider? How many of these did you wind up reporting?* If an investigator tries enough variables in a kind of statistical fishing expedition, he or she is almost bound to find something, true or untrue.

In cause-and-effect and other studies, ask: *Has there been any reanalysis of the data?* "Results, if possible, should be method-independent," Greenberg believes. "You should recalculate and see if the results hold up."

A word of caution: Questions about multivariate analyses or reanalyses can be tricky. Whether or not·to do one kind of analysis or reanalysis or none at all is often a matter of dispute among authorities. Launch the subject with some humility. A reasoned answer, affirmative or negative, may tell you more than the answer's precise content.

In studies of medical treatments or preventives: *How did you know or decide when your patients were cured or improved? Were there explicit, objective outcome criteria?* That is, were there firm measurements or test results rather than physicians' observations in interviews, physical examinations, or chart reviews, all techniques highly subject to great *observer variation* and inaccuracy? If improvement or relief from pain—a particularly soft (hard to quantify) outcome measure—had to be judged by observers: *Was there some systematic way of making an assessment?*

If two or more groups were compared for survival, was their starting

*point the same at onset? At diagnosis? At start of treatment? Were they
judged by the same disease definitions at the start and the same measures of
severity and outcome?*

*Did the intervention have the good results that were intended? Has
there been an evaluation to see whether it was a useful result?*
Investigators often report that a drug or other measure has
lowered blood cholesterol levels. Fine, but were they able to
show that it reduced the number of heart attacks? Or was reduc-
tion of a supposed risk factor itself taken to mean the hoped-for
outcome? That may often be necessary, but the issue should be
discussed.

Investigators once reported that a new heart drug reduced
the number of recurrent myocardial infarctions (heart attacks),
fatal and nonfatal. But total mortality for all causes was higher
in the treated group than in a placebo group.

Public health officials may announce the success of a cam-
paign to take high blood pressure measurements: X number of
people were found to be hypertensive and were referred to their
doctors. But how many went to their doctors? How many of
those received optimum treatment? Were their blood pressures
reduced? (If they were, the evidence is strong that they should
suffer fewer strokes.)

In short: *What was the bottom line? Did you really do any good?*

*To whom do your results apply? Can they be generalized to a larger
population? Are your patients like the average doctor's patients? Is there any
basis in these findings for any patient to ask his or her doctor for a change in
treatment?* Clinic populations, hospital populations, and the
"worst cases" are not necessarily typical of patients in general,
and improper generalization is unfortunately common in the
medical literature.

Again and again, in many of the cases cited in this chapter,
ask: *Do other studies back you up? Are your results consistent with other
clinical and experimental findings? Have your results been repeated or*

confirmed or supported by other studies? Or have only you been able to get these results?

Virtually no single study proves anything. Two or 4 or 15 studies add credence, especially if the diagnostic and outcome criteria and the people studied are similar. Consistency of results in humans, animals, and laboratory tests also adds credence.

One scientist warns, however, "You have to be wary about a grab bag of studies with different populations and different circumstances." To which Harvard's Mosteller adds, "Yes, be wary, but consistency across such differences cheers me up." And Dr. John Bailar tells us that, despite possible pitfalls, *"meta-analysis* of several low power reports"—that is, statistically analyzing and integrating their results—*"may* come to stronger conclusions than any one of them alone" (italics mine).[8]

Mostly just good-sense questions? Of course. Some of the most important questions of all for a reporter to ponder are these: *What do I think? Do the conclusions make sense to me?* Do the data really justify the conclusions? If this person has extrapolated beyond the evidence, has he or she explained why and made sense?*

Does the investigator frankly document or discuss the possible biases and flaws in the study? A good scientific paper should do so. *Does the investigator admit that the conclusion may be tentative or equivocal?* Dr. Robert Boruch of Northwestern University says, "It requires audacity and some courage to say, 'I don't know.'"[9] *Do the authors use qualifying phrases?* If such phrases are important, we are bound to include them in any responsible story.

Ask the investigators themselves: *How much weight should your work be given? Is it really firm? And how important?* An experienced science reporter says, "I have found that good researchers generally have an honest and proportionate view of their

---

*Frederick Mosteller disagrees with my occasional reference to good sense or common sense. If something is a commonsense idea, he says, "surely all would have thought of it. So it must be uncommon sense after all." He makes good sense.

own work's importance." But there are many exceptions.

Ask others in the same field: *How do other informed people regard this report — and these investigators? Are they speaking in their own area of expertise, or have they shown real mastery if they have ventured outside it? Have their past results generally held up? And what are some good questions I can ask them?* True, a lot of brilliant and original work has been pooh-poohed for a time by others. Still, scientists survive only by eventually convincing their colleagues.

More formally: *Has there been a review of the data and conclusions by any disinterested parties?* Some major clinical studies are reviewed by independent second parties or committees. Reports of the National Academy of Sciences must pass muster by a review committee.

Has there been peer review of the material? That is, has it been examined by referees who were sent the article by a journal editor?

And, a very important question: *Has the work been published or accepted by a reputable journal? If not, why not?* The *New England Journal of Medicine* prints only 15 percent of the papers submitted to it (many, of course, are rejected because they are not of enough interest to the journal's readers). Many have been given at medical or scientific meetings, yet do not pass peer reviewers' or the editors' muster. Most are eventually published elsewhere, many in good journals. But there are journals and journals.

In science as a whole, including biology and often basic medical sciences, *Science* and the British *Nature* are indispensable. In general medicine and clinical science at the physician's level, the best, most useful journals are probably *New England Journal of Medicine, Journal of the American Medical Association, Annals of Internal Medicine, Canadian Medical Journal, Journal of Clinical Investigation,* and the British *Lancet* and *British Medical Journal.* There are many equally good specialty journals as well as mediocre ones. In epidemiology, three good sources are *American Journal of Epidemiology, Journal of Chronic Diseases,* and *Preventive Medicine.* Ask people in any field: What are the most reliable journals, those where you would want your work published?

Some of the most valuable journals to a medical reporter are not journals of original publication but review publications like *Family Practice* and *Hospital Practice,* which mainly print summary articles for practitioners. With some strong exceptions, the free-circulation—also known as controlled-circulation—journals and medical magazines, which depend wholly on advertising for revenue, are not as rigorously screened as the traditional journals. They are often on top of the news, however. All journals print clinkers sometimes. "Scientific journals are records of work, not of revealed truth," says the *New England Journal's* Dr. Arnold Relman.[10]

Read the entire journal article yourself, if there is one. Ask the investigator for a copy or phone the journal. Or, assuming the article has already been published, look for it at a medical library, which can be found at any medical college, most good hospitals, and the headquarters of many county medical societies. Too many news releases tout articles that read far more conservatively than the PR version. Many scientists go much further in interviews or news conferences than they are willing to go in their articles. A reporter asked a scientist, "Does peer review of an article put you at ease?" He said, "It should help put you at greater ease, but nothing puts me at ease until I've read the article."

Most reporters can't be scientific referees, but *when you read an article, look for the following:*

• A credit or footnote indicating collaboration with a statistician, and a paragraph describing the method of statistical analysis and its outcomes, such as P value or confidence level, power to detect treatment effects, and so on. If they're in place, you can at least assume that some effort was made to apply the rigors of statistical analysis. If they're missing, should you beware? Sometimes. Sometimes the statistician is a coauthor whose specialty isn't identified. And some investigators are well versed in statistics.

• Tables and figures that tell the same story as the conclusions. Sometimes they don't. One statistician told reporters,

"Don't assume that someone can interpret his own data. You may do better." And "muddle around in the footnotes and appendices," Mosteller advises. "You might find a few horrors. That's how people found out that a much publicized study of public and private schools included only about 12 private, non-parochial schools."

• Other things described in this chapter, such as the protocol and study design, the criteria for admitting and randomizing subjects, the therapy actually received (in contrast to that planned in the protocol), blinding, complications, loss to follow-up, follow-up time, and any discussion of reservations or weaknesses.

Ask, when appropriate: *Where did the money to support the study come from?* Many honest investigators are financed by companies that may profit from the outcome. So are some dishonest or self-deluding investigators. But the peddler of a biased point of view is as likely to be an antiestablishment crusader — or an academic ladder-climber — as a corporate darling. Perhaps the best question to ask yourself is, Is this investigator a scientist or a salesman? In any case, the public should know any pertinent connections.

"What proportion of papers will satisfy [all] the requirements for scientific proof and clinical applicability?" Sackett writes, "Not very many. . . . After all, there are only a handful of ways to do a study properly but a thousand ways to do it wrong."[11]

Despite impeccable design, some studies yield answers that turn out to be wrong. Some fail for lack of understanding of physiology and disease. Even the soundest studies may provoke controversy. No study settles anything for all time.

And according to Sackett, some "may meet considerable resistance when they discredit the only treatment currently available. . . . Clinicians may still elect to do something, even if it is of no demonstrable benefit. Study results may be rejected, regardless of their merit, if they threaten the prestige or livelihood of their audience."

Reporters need to tread a narrow path between believing everything and believing nothing. Also — we are reporters — some of the controversies make important stories.

Tests and Testing

6

DO physicians always know what they're doing when they administer tests? Stanford's Dr. Eugene Robin says many tests "have not been properly evaluated and in fact may be useless or harmful." He asks, "Is it common practice in medicine to perform careful clinical trials before introducing tests that can affect the welfare of masses of patients? Sadly, the answer is no."[1]

A good test should detect both health and disease and do so with high accuracy. The measures of the value of a *clinical test,* one used for medical diagnosis, are *sensitivity* and *specificity,* or, simply, the ability to avoid *false negatives* and *false positives. Sensitivity* is how well a test identifies a disease or condition in those who have it—how well it *avoids false negatives,* or missed cases. If 100 people with a condition are tested and 90 test positive, the test's sensitivity is 90 percent. *Specificity* is how well a test identifies those who do not have the disease or condition—how well it *rules out false positives,* or mistaken identifications. If 100 healthy people are tested and 90 test negative, the test's specificity is 90 percent.

Sensitivity, in short, tells us about *disease present. Specificity* tells us about *disease absent.* A highly unspecific test will produce many false positives; a highly insensitive test, many false negatives. Almost every test produces some of both, and the two qualities — such is nature — are *inversely related,* for there is always an overlap. The more sensitive you make a test to try to find every case, the less specific it will be and the more false positives you will get. The more specific you make it to try to avoid false labeling, the less sensitive it will be and the more false negatives you will get.

As a born layman, I find it easy to get confused about these terms. ("So do we professionals!" a noted medical statistician comments.) Actually — while it is important to understand the concept, the inherent conflict between the two qualities, and the fact that tests are not perfect — almost all a reporter need ask the person who unveils a new test for AIDS or cancer or diabetes is this:

How many false negatives and false positives do you get? How do you know this? Have you done an adequate trial — judged by some of the tests in the last chapter? Here, one quality, the *definition* of the medical condition under study, is crucial. A new test should be tried and assessed by blinded observers in subjects chosen by some *definitive diagnoses* — that is, by surgery, biopsy, long-term follow-up, or other precise method — as patients who have the condition being sought. And it should be tried as well in healthy subjects, and often it should be tried in some who have a condition frequently confused with the one being studied.

How well should a test do in avoiding false negatives and false positives? That may depend on its goal. If the main aim is not to miss some serious condition, it may shoot for high sensitivity to pick up every possible case. If the main concern is avoiding false positives in a disease doctors can't do much about anyway, one may opt for more specificity.

Doubt was expressed about some tests for strep throat, because in 25 reports their sensitivity ranged from a reasonably acceptable 93 percent to an unacceptably low 65 percent. In short, there were too many false negatives. A study group evaluated home pregnancy-testing kits whose maker claimed they detected pregnancy 95 to 98 percent of the time. Testing them in

144 pregnant women, the study group found them only 75.6 percent sensitive—one false negative in every four tests.[2]

Other problems in clinical testing:

How valid—how accurate—is the test? How closely do its results reflect a true condition? Epidemiologist Gary Friedman's example: Measuring a heart rate by putting your fingers on someone's wrist—taking a radial pulse—would lack validity for some patients with certain disturbances in heart rhythm because some of their heartbeats produce too weak a pulse to be felt at the wrist.[3]

How reliable, or reproducible, is the test? Does a series of observations produce the same or nearly the same result? "Validity" and "reliability" are another set of easily confused terms. To a statistician or experimenter, *validity* means accuracy; *reliability,* how reproducible a test or experiment is when repeated. If the results of a test typically vary, it must be repeated, perhaps several times, to get a mean and a more reliable result. Some results may vary through no fault of the test but simply because they reflect different conditions: say, your blood pressure when you're relaxed and when you're tense.

All tests are subject to error. Results can be affected by diet, drugs, exposure of a blood sample to light, a malfunctioning instrument, or a cockeyed observer.

What about tests that produce not numbers but some subjective result like an image or pattern or human assessment—an X ray, a tendon reflex, a heart murmur, the wavy lines of an electrocardiogram? Different observers may vary widely in their interpretations. In a classic study an investigator had 10 "qualified" persons examine, or "read," each of 1,807 chest X rays for "true positive" abnormals or "true negative" normals, as unanimously defined by a separate panel. Each reader failed to recognize a third of the abnormal X rays, on the average (but, more acceptably, called only 2 percent of the negatives normal).[4]

The lesson, incidentally, if you're a patient: Be cautious about letting yourself be sentenced to a dire diagnosis on the basis of any one test (although one bone marrow examination may indicate leukemia; one X ray may clearly show a fracture or kidney stone). Similarly, few tests, however negative the result, are sure enough to give us a "clean bill of health." For example, in January 1987 a usually excellent radio news program said tests on President Reagan had ruled out any spread of his earlier cancer. Even if such tests were 100 percent sensitive, which they were not, they could not rule out cancer. Its spread is often undetectable and therefore unmeasurable, though it may later manifest itself. Such tests could only show that no spread of cancer had been found. In assessing health or disease, a good physician considers the results of a combination of several tests, as well as physical signs, symptoms, your behavior, and your history.

There is also a potential trap in the word "normal." Some testers use it to mean average or statistically typical; some to mean healthy or desirable or free of disease. "Within the normal range," a phrase often used, can mean little unless explained. If someone tells you your serum cholesterol — the amount of cholesterol in your blood — is 210 (milligrams per deciliter), that may be average for adult Americans, but it is too high to be optimal in the view of physicians who think it's associated with an elevated risk of atherosclerosis, or clogged arteries.

Similarly, "abnormal" may just mean that a particular laboratory finds you're in the top or bottom 5 or 10 percent of test results at that lab or some group of labs. Thus "abnormal" might or might not mean anything clinically, anything affecting your health.

Ask: *Does "normal" mean average, or does it mean okay? Does "abnormal" mean atypical or unhealthy?*

In addition to clinical tests to investigate some complaint, there are *screening tests* of normal persons, designed to pick out those who might have some condition but need further examination to confirm it. Examples: routine Pap smears, mammograms, the tuberculin test to find those exposed to the TB bacillus, multiphasic testing for many conditions.

A good screening test should be sufficiently specific, sensitive, accurate, and predictive. The *predictive value* is the proportion of all positive tests that are from truly diseased or (if that is the test's purpose) susceptible people — those who will be positive on further, definitive testing, not merely positives who turn out to be negative. Screening tests are necessarily a rough screen in some cases. In some screening tests most of the "positives" will turn out not to have the disease.

The predictive value is a function of specificity, sensitivity, and *prevalence* (the actual case rate that is discovered; see page 76). A test for a very rare disease may be high in specificity and sensitivity yet have a low predictive value and turn up few cases among the so-called positives. A screening test should not be so rough that it exposes hundreds or thousands of actually healthy people to worry and expense, to possibly harmful further testing by chemical or invasive means, and to possibly harmful surgery or other treatment.

Studies that try to assess screening tests can easily be deceiving. People who take better care of themselves — or, perversely, those most likely to have the disease — may self-select themselves as test subjects. A test like mammography to detect breast cancer may pick up a number of women who have very early cancers that would not have been detected otherwise until later. Fine, but when they are treated, they may turn out to have deceptively longer-than-average survivals only because of the early detection. Those who struggle to assess such programs call this *lead-time bias.*

Many authorities think society should forgo screening programs unless a test of demonstrated value attacks an important health problem that doctors can do something about at a cost within reason.

Drugs and Drug Trials

Do you think physicians always know what they're doing when they prescribe drugs? Many authorities recommend mistrusting any doctor, however convinced, who says, "Don't worry. I've been using this drug for years, and I've never seen these adverse reactions you read about." By one calculation, "the individual physician is in a functional sense 'blind' to treatment-related risk" that occurs any less commonly than once in about 200 patients.[5] Drugs have been withdrawn or forced into restricted use because of adverse reactions in the range of 1 in 1,000 to 1 in 30,000.

Are such drug withdrawals good or bad for society and for patients? The Food and Drug Administration, which judges drugs, is alternately attacked as the protector of venal drug companies foisting harmful drugs on the public and as the citadel of needless regulation that denies good drugs to patients and profits to business.

In fact, many pharmaceutical firms have poor records in informing the FDA and the public of reports of adverse reactions. And physicians, sufferers from some diseases, and parents of sick children have had to lobby the FDA and Congress to pry out a few drugs that timid federal officials feared to release, having been attacked in the past for prematurely approving drugs that turned out to have undetected adverse effects. The best course is not always easy to decide. If you're the 1 patient in 30,000 who is dead, you're very dead. But will withdrawing the drug cause many more deaths in people who might have been saved by it?

By and large, all that was said in the last chapter on questions reporters can ask applies to drugs and medications. When a scientist or a company comes forth with a new drug or a new use for an old one, ask: *How do you know it works? What is your evidence?* And ask questions about the studies. Warning: You are not likely to find many of the answers in most of the elaborate press kits that accompany the commercial release of many drugs.

An important thing to understand in reporting news of drug trials is that, by FDA rules, they are conducted in phases, hurdles that must be leaped before a drug can win FDA approval. In a *Phase I* trial a new drug is tested in humans for the first time. It has already been studied first *in vitro* ("in glass"), in test tubes (or petri dishes or beakers or flasks), then *in vivo* ("in something living"), in animals. In Phase I, the investigator tests for human toxicity and other physiological responses, seeking a dosage range and schedule of acceptable toxicity. The subjects are usually small groups of healthy persons. The doses studied are at first small, then gradually larger.

In *Phase II,* the drug is tried in as many as 100 to 200 patients to establish dosages that might do some good. Again, there may be studies of various doses, schedules, and safety margins. Some Phase II studies are, like Phase I's, *open studies,* with doctors and patients knowing that a new compound is being tested. Other Phase II studies are randomized and blinded.

Phase III means *a full-scale clinical trial or trials* to pit the drug against other treatments or no treatment. This is the last step in this series of steps that may take years and typically involve hundreds or even thousands of patients or normal subjects before winning FDA approval. Ideally, Phase III trials should be fully randomized and blinded studies comparing comparable groups of patients and subjects. For reasons of necessity or expense, they are sometimes less perfect: sometimes crossover studies (the same patients getting one treatment, then another), sometimes trials comparing the patients with past medical records (historical controls).

Differences in physiological response from patient to patient, spontaneous recoveries, the placebo effect, in which many patients respond to anything they are given—all these make drug testing at its best something less than a gold-plated assurance that a drug is now safe and effective.

But the greatest problem of all is that 1,000, 5,000, or even 15,000 patients are few compared with the many more thousands or even millions who may have to get a drug before all its effects and their frequency become known. The real safety test of a drug is its use by doctors in general on patients in general.

It is in this "big but poorly controlled experiment," by one description, that the life-threatening events often turn up.

Among the largest premarketing test groups to date have been the 15,000 women given the first oral contraceptive and the 20,000 people given the first oral antidiabetes drug. But if a drug produces an unwanted reaction in only 1 in 25,000 patients, it would have to be given to 250,000 patients to produce about 10 such reactions.

The antibiotic chloramphenicol (Chloromycetin) was approved and given to some 5 million people before the FDA decided that it caused serious blood disorders and death in 1 in perhaps 24,000 to 40,000 patients. The FDA then limited the drug's *approved indications* to a small number of infections, most commonly typhoid fever, and, when no other drug works, some eye, ear, and skin disorders. Many doctors who said they had never seen an adverse reaction continued using the drug more indiscriminately for years, and reports of deaths kept piling up.

There are actually no good figures on adverse reactions to most of the drugs in general use. Less than 5 percent of such reactions, it is estimated, ever get reported to the FDA by physicians, despite exhortations to do so. A physician may legally use any licensed drug for any purpose, but he does so at the peril of a malpractice suit if the use is unapproved. And hundreds of doctors, mainly in academic medical centers, are using scores of unlicensed, experimental drugs on patients under FDA investigational permits.

You can read about licensed prescription drugs, including their noncapitalized generic or scientific names, their capitalized trade names, and their possible side effects and approved uses, in the annual *Physicians' Desk Reference,* or *PDR*—and about many nonprescription drugs in the *PDR for Non-Prescription Drugs.* But both are commercial organs in which only companies that choose to do so describe their products. And prescription drugs are described in the language approved by FDA as the *labeling* or *package insert* usually seen only by pharmacists, not by patients. Reading about all the possible side effects of a drug can be frightening—at times, perhaps unnecessarily so. Dr. Gary Friedman notes that "companies tend to include every possible side effect that has been reported, probably to protect themselves."[6] Just the same, a reporter writing about a drug should read the full text.

Animals as Models for Us

Animals are the most common research subjects of all. Mice and rats are tested by the millions, other animals by the hundreds or thousands.

Animals are often much like people in their reactions, and often very different. The challenge to scientists is to pick the right *animal model* for the subject—the human disease or risk or physiological change—being studied. Armadillos are reasonable models for the study of leprosy, cats for deafness, chimpanzees for AIDS, mice for cancer and epilepsy, rats for diabetes and aging, and dogs for many conditions, but no animal is a completely satisfactory model for any human disease.

Cortisone gives cleft palate to mice but not men. A dose of morphine that can kill a human merely anesthetizes a dog. Arsenic doesn't induce cancer in animals but does in man. A late colleague of mine would toss many an animal research story aside with the comment "Mice are not men." In some ways, however, animals are superior to human beings as research subjects. No experimenter can control all human variables, but a scientist can select an inbred strain of mice with common genetics and keep all or most conditions of the experiment constant.

True, dosages in an animal experiment usually must be far higher than in typical human exposures, even given the difference in body weight. It takes both large dosages and large numbers of subjects to get an answer in mice, which live only a few years, in a reasonable time at an affordable cost. And you might hear someone scoff at the fact that rats developed bladder cancers only after daily exposure to the amount of saccharin found in 800 diet sodas. That may sound unreasonable, yet it can be one useful fact in a reasonable assessment of saccharin risks.

Animal studies are not without possible biases. Animals, like people, vary from day to day in their physiology and behavior. The position of a cage in a room may affect response; careful researchers rotate cages to avoid this *cage effect*. Animals sometimes have undetected infections. There can even be an analogy to the placebo effect: a *handling effect*, which some researchers believe is due to "a physiological response from letting them know that we care."

The most difficult problem is the problem of extrapolating from animals to man. Animals can nonetheless alert us to potential uses for drugs and potential problems of chemicals and other agents. There are many classic animal experiments. In 1945 Howard Florey and Ernst Chain infected mice with streptococci, then injected some of them with the new experimental drug penicillin. All of the untreated mice were dead by the next day; all the treated mice lived.

In extrapolating from animals to man, said a 1984 scientific panel, "the characterization of human risk always requires interdisciplinary evaluation of the entire array of data"—laboratory, animal, and human—"on a case by case basis."[7]

In short, it requires human judgment. And the reporter asking a scientist about an animal experiment should ask much the same questions one would ask about a human experiment: *Were there controls? Were there possible biases? What were the numbers? What is the statistical significance of the result?* And: *What is the biological or medical significance? Is this animal a good model for what might happen in humans? Do you think we can extrapolate? Is there a possible application to human beings?*

Vital Statistics: The Numbers of Life and Health

7

I said to a patient who was an undertaker, "I'm curious. How did you happen to pick me as your physician?" He replied: "Nothing to it. I checked the records and found you wrote the fewest death certificates."

—Dr. Philip R. Alper in *Medical Economics*

"Jes' don't die, I guess."

—A southern centenarian when asked by a TV reporter, "What should we do to live a long time?"

VITAL STATISTICS are the statistics of life, health, disease, and death, the statistics of much that we hold dear and much that we fear. They tell us of the burden of illness and its costs. They measure our progress against disease and premature death, or should do so if properly applied.

They are much misapplied, misused, and misunderstood. We who report the news often misunderstand them or ignore them. They seem dull. We prefer to hear about ideas, subjects, people. Yet these statistics can yield fascinating stories if we learn something of their power and limits and the rather special vocabulary of human lives.

The science of statistics was launched in large part by a reportorially minded 17th-century Englishman, John Graunt, who took it upon himself to look at some records the crown had been collecting but not interpreting. From 1592 to 1594 and starting again in 1603, it had published a weekly Bill of Mortality for the London area, listing christenings, burials, and causes of death (including Affrighted, Childbed, Dead in the Street and Starved, Executed and prest to death, French Pox, Grief, Teeth, Worms, and Suddenly).

Graunt began counting and tabulating. He identified the three leading causes of death for 1632: Chrisomes and Infants (chrisomes were white robes for child christenings or burials, hence infants), Consumption (tuberculosis and probably cancer and other wasting disease), and Fever. He noted the years of plague epidemics, developed rates and proportions as ways to describe what he saw, and pointed out how such data might be used to spot problems. "There is much pleasure," he wrote, "in deducing so many abstruse, and unexpected inferences."[1] Not until the mid-19th century did registration of births and causes of death become at all regular in both the United States and Britain, but Graunt's rates remain central to measuring nature's continuing experiment that is life.

A *rate,* to a statistician, is a specific kind of proportion. A percentage is a proportion too, but a rate always expresses its numerator and its stated or implied denominator or baseline as "so many per so many." A rate is a way of describing a group. It answers the question, Compared with whom? or Compared with what?

The two most commonly used medical rates — *incidence* and *prevalence* — are often confused, even in the medical literature. An *incidence rate* is the number of persons who get a disease (or the occurrence of any event) divided by the total number at risk (or total given population) per unit of time. For example, the incidence rate of disease A is 3 percent a year in the United States, or the incidence of disease B was 5,000 last year in this country. Incidence measures only new cases or, strictly, new cases that are diagnosed. Often the true incidence can only be estimated.

The *mortality rate* is the incidence of *deaths* per unit of time in a community, nation, or group. A *morbidity rate* is the equivalent incidence of a particular *disease* or, often, all illness.

Incidence counts only new cases, but the *prevalence rate* of a disease or characteristic is the total case rate, both new and old, in a given population at a given time. It is the total number of persons affected at that time divided by the total population.

If incidence is like an entering class, prevalence is the whole school. Examples: The prevalence rate of condition A in the screening exam at the plant was 1 percent. The prevalence of influenza was 10 percent in the nursing home last January 1. The prevalence of condition B in new mothers in the first 24 hours after childbirth is 2 percent. (The word "rate" is often assumed in many incidence and prevalence rates.)

Case rate is a term sometimes used to mean a disease's prevalence rate, with *new case rate* referring to the incidence. But be careful—all these terms are often used loosely or carelessly.

Students of mortality sometimes rank causes of death not by simple totals alone but by *years of life lost:* the number of deaths multiplied by the number of years lost from the normal life expectancies of the victims. Accidents are the leading cause of years of life lost, since most accident victims are young and are deprived of many expected years.

Crude Rates versus Rates That Compare

We said that rates answer the question, Compared with what? There are several ways of describing populations or groups so they can be compared.

• A *crude rate*—whether an incidence, mortality, or prevalence rate—simply tells you the number of cases or whatever in a population. It is important to know, but it's no help if you want to know where the disease is concentrated.

• A *group-specific rate* can more tellingly state the number of cases in some subgroup, that is, what proportion of what group is affected.

• An *age-specific rate* or an *age- and sex-specific rate* is often given in five- or ten-year groupings.

• A *case-fatality rate* is the number of persons dying of a disease divided by the total number who have it. This may be stated per unit of time or simply as the proportion who eventually die of the condition.

• The *maternal mortality rate* is the number of maternal deaths attributed to childbirth in a year divided by total live births (only live births are considered because stillbirths, which really should be included, are not fully counted and legally registered).

• An *attack rate* is the cumulative count of new cases (in relation to a total population) without specifying a unit of time, though it is commonly used in connection with a specific *epidemic* or—a term with a little less emotional charge—*outbreak* of a disease.

• When you need to compare two groups and they differ in some important way—say, in age—you need an *adjusted* or *standardized rate,* one that uses some method to calculate what would happen if the two groups were comparable in age distribution. One method of arriving at an *age-adjusted rate,* one of the rates most commonly seen, is to choose some *standard population*—the U.S. population in a particular year, for example—and calculate the number of cases that would occur if the population you are looking at had the same distribution. The age-adjusted rate for Florida, then, would tell you what Florida's rate would be if that state wasn't a retirement mecca but had a more normal distribution of younger people.

True, you are now in one way dealing with a contrived rate that does not truly describe the population. For that, you need either the crude rate or some group-specific rates or both. Yet for many purposes an adjusted rate gives you a clearer picture.

One statistician says, "I think group-specific rates give you the clearest picture of a disease. But say you want to compare two cities. If you just want to know the prevalence of a disease in the two, you should know the crude rates—after all, they tell you how big a problem each city has. But if you want to know why the two cities differ, you must adjust, ideally, by age, sex, race, income, and often occupation. And you'll know even more if you also compare the group-specific rates in the two."

A common error, incidentally, in the media — including the Washington, D.C., media — is to compare the nation's capital, which is a city, with the 50 states just because it is necessarily listed that way in many tables. You might accurately but misleadingly report that "Washington, D.C., has a higher rate of disease than any state," when you should compare Washington with other cities, which often have higher rates of many unsavory conditions than their states as a whole, generally because they have more poor people.

If you did not age-adjust U.S. cancer rates when comparing them from decade to decade, you would not know that crude cancer rates have been on the increase, in largest part because people have been living long enough to get cancer instead of dying from other diseases. Also, if you did not, for some uses, subtract the effect of smoking in causing lung cancer from the total cancer rate, you would think cancer as a whole has been on the rise as steeply as that grievously epidemic kind of cancer.

Other Ways to Compare

An adjusted rate gives you what statisticians call an *expected rate*, compared with the actual *observed rate*. As Friedman points out, you might want to compare the lung cancer rate in a group of smokers with that in some nonsmokers of various ages. You want to compare the results of smoking, not age, so you age-adjust the nonsmokers' lung cancer rate to the rate you'd *expect* if they were the same age as the smokers. You can now more accurately see the effect of cigarettes on the smokers.[2]

You'll sometimes see a reference to the *magnitude* of a difference between two groups. That's just its size. Say one group has 100 more cases of a disease than another, or one has a 50 percent greater rate. Those figures are the magnitudes of the difference. (Scientists in many fields often say *by an order of magnitude* when they mean either 2 times greater or 10 times greater, depending on the scientist, the context, and usage in that field. And in astronomy "magnitude" is defined as a ratio of 2:512; a star of the first magnitude is 2:512 times as bright as one of the second magnitude, and so on. See page 20 for use of *by a power of* as a measure of magnitude.)

A difference between two incidence or prevalence rates can be called an *excess rate* or *excess risk* — and an *attributable risk* if there is a difference in some variable, like cigarette smoking, strongly believed to cause the difference. Investigators like to say the guilty variable has a "causal role," a good phrase to avoid in print since a typo so often changes it to a "casual" role.

Two rates can also be usefully compared by calculating the ratio of one to the other, that is, dividing one by the other. This gives you the *relative risk,* or *risk ratio.* If disease A occurs in 200 cases per 100,000 in group X and in 50 per 100,000 in group Y, group X's risk is four times greater than group Y's. This is commonly expressed as a relative risk of 4 in a paragraph or table listing the relative risks for various groups. You'll more often see a lower number for a relative risk, such as 1.3 or 1.5 — that is, a 30 or 50 percent chance of disease, death, exposure, or whatever. As we've seen before, a reported relative risk that low may or may not signal a problem, given the unreliability of observation and of many studies.

Reporting Hospital Death Rates

After you've been sick, you get well or you don't, you survive or you don't. These fates, good or bad, are called *outcomes. Outcome rates* or measures — increasingly important in assessing both the medical and the cost effectiveness of medical care — can include *improvement, recovery, cure, failure* (the patient didn't get well), *complications, disability, survival,* and *death,* or *mortality,* rates.

The government's Medicare-Medicaid agency, the Health Care Financing Administration (HCFA), has begun publishing death rates among Medicare patients — about 40 percent of all patients—in American hospitals. Their care is also monitored by a national network of Professional Review Organizations (PROs) who must make their studies public, on request. At this writing, one state PRO (California's) has begun regular publication of California hospitals' death rates. In some states other agencies have started collecting and sometimes releasing similar information. All this creates a new obligation for the media: to seek and interpret these life and death figures.

We may get them for all hospitals or just for outliers, those with rates well above or below expected or predicted rates based on national averages. But these rates alone still may not tell you which hospitals may be life-savers and which may be death traps. The rates may have been adjusted for some variables—such as age, sex, previous hospitalization, and the presence of various co-morbidities (illnesses other than the main one causing the admission)—to try to make one hospital's rates comparable with another's. Barring vast future improvements, however, they probably will not have been adequately adjusted for the most important variable of all, severity of illness—or very likely for other aspects of patient mix, perhaps including socioeconomic status and other characteristics that can affect medical outcomes.

For this reason, a mere list of hospitals and mortality rates will not tell you that hospital A's patients may be far sicker than hospital B's. Or poorer, which generally means sicker. Or homeless or without family or other resources, so they cannot readily be transferred to a nursing home or hospice or their own homes and thus often die in the hospital. Or hospital A's patients may to a larger extent be emergency admissions, which also means sicker. A trauma center, a hospital that specializes in burns, a tertiary-care center where other hospitals send their most complicated cases—all may have higher death rates than a simpler community hospital.

The reporter's obligation remains: to try to make sense of these figures, to try to tell the public where it has the best chance of coming out alive, or, at the least, to name those hospitals whose statistics should make patients ask doctors: "Should I really go to this hospital?"

Experience so far shows that virtually every hospital official, confronted with a report of high death rates, will say, "Our patients are sicker." But many studies show that there are indeed true differences in care from hospital to hospital. Dr. Henry Krakauer, an HCFA official, has estimated that 50 percent of the higher mortality rates may be caused by inferior care; an academic authority has put the figure at "maybe half, maybe 40 percent." A former HCFA official has said, "I don't think there's anyone in the health field in this country who would randomly enter any hospital for major surgery. I would choose where I went."

How can we help the public choose? The following are some possible questions for reporters to ask hospitals, PROs, state health officials in states that monitor hospitals, and—publicly or privately—doctors, who often know where the bodies are buried.

The first question to ask anyone—and to ask yourself while looking at the figures—may be this: *How can any of these statistics be of use to patients?* Do any of these numbers show or even hint at anything that a potential patient should know?

A question to ask anyone familiar with the local medical and hospital picture: *What questions should I ask about these numbers to try to get the best information for patients? Do they tell me anything that the medical community, but not the public, has been aware of?* This hospital with high operative death rates—is it a surgery mill known for its bad work?

How do you account for the fact that this hospital has a high overall mortality rate—or a high mortality rate for coronary bypass operations (or any other procedure or illness)? Authorities say that overall hospital death rates are usually less useful in comparing hospitals than death rates by illness or procedure. Surgical death rates may be the most reliable indicators, though they too may or may not indicate good or bad care. There may be at least a few procedures, however, for which results should be roughly similar in almost all hospitals, given good care. These include results in coronary artery bypass grafting (the bypass operation for heart patients), prostate operations, and cholecystectomies (gall bladder operations). Unfortunately, HCFA's most recent release at this writing included no surgical results. A reporter may still try to get this kind of information from one source or another.

When you are told, "These patients are sicker [or whatever], so the results can't be up to the expected rate," *Shouldn't the public still take notice — and at least ask some more questions and possibly be alarmed — if the mortality rate is two or even three or four times the expected rate?* This has been the case for a number of hospitals. The greater the difference, the higher the index of suspicion.

When you are told that a hospital's patients are different — poorer or sicker or more emergency room cases: *Can you back this up with statistics, including statistics about this hospital's population compared with those of other hospitals in the area?*

When one hospital's results are poorer than others': *Is your care really equal to hospital B's? Were the AMI* (acute myocardial infarction, or heart attack) *patients equally well monitored? Is the CCU* (coronary care unit) *as well staffed and equipped? Were complications appropriately treated? Are your nurses overworked? Is your equipment up to date?* A reporter can benefit by previously asking the right doctor this question: What are some important things we might suspect if the figures look questionable?

When you are told that a rate is unfavorably high because of patient population: *Can you point to any hospitals with similar patient mixes with equally unfavorable-sounding rates in or out of your area? Or is this hospital one of very few? Did some do better? How did they manage it?*

If you are told that a hospital is an academic medical center with many referred, very sick patients or a public hospital with many poor: *What about these figures that show that some hospitals in the same class — X University Hospital and Y City Hospital — manage to treat tough patients and keep their death rates down?*

If you are told that the mortality rate is high because the

hospital has a policy of not sending patients home to die unless there are family and home resources: *How can this hospital afford to do that in the face of limits that reimburse it only for an average number of days of care? Does it pay for the unreimbursed differences? Don't many hospitals succeed in transferring such patients to a hospice or a nursing home?* Does this say something about the hospital's need for improvement in its social services or discharge planning or cooperation with other community resources?

If you are still troubled about a hospital's apparently high mortality rate: *If I were a patient, shouldn't I at the least go to my doctor and say, "What do you know about this situation? How do you account for these figures? Would you go to this hospital or send someone in your family there? Have you ever done so? Should I go there? Is it the very best place for me to go, the place where I will have the best chance for recovery?"*

If you are told that a hospital's apparently high mortality rate for coronary bypass surgery (or whatever) does not mean it is not giving superior care: *Is this hospital doing enough of these procedures to be one of the most experienced and successful hospitals? Or is it treating so few patients of this kind that its physicians and staff can't possibly get enough experience to be among the most skilled?*

Dr. Sidney Wolfe, director of the Health Research Group founded by Ralph Nader, discussed the first HCFA release of hospital mortality rates in March 1986: Of 33 hospitals with an elevated coronary bypass mortality rate, 24 were doing fewer than 100 operations a year. The lowest mortality rate among them was 14 percent. "That's just unconscionable," he said. Conversely, the hospitals with lower-than-expected mortality rates, all under 2 percent (a rate seven times lower), did more than 300 bypass operations each year on Medicare patients alone. "What this tells us is that hospitals that are doing very few of these operations, or any others, shouldn't be doing them at all," Wolfe said.

Many authorities agree. Many say a patient shouldn't have coronary artery surgery at a hospital that does fewer than 200 or 300 such operations a year, at all ages. The same principle applies for many other procedures, including: hip surgery, prostate surgery, appendectomies and other intestinal operations, and treatment of heart attacks. "Hospitals with high mortality rates and low volumes should be of special concern," says Dr. John Bunker of Stanford.

When a hospital has an alarming-sounding mortality rate: *Has it examined patient records or any medical or surgical practices? Has the hospital made any changes, or will it at least be thinking about changes, in the medical staff? medical staff privileges* (who can do what kind of surgery)? *other operating room, intensive care, postsurgical care or emergency room staff? equipment? training? Shouldn't it be making or considering changes? Would you call it remiss if it does not?*

Is this hospital planning to continue giving this kind of care, or is it considering referring such cases to a regional or other center?

"Bad-apple" physicians, not the hospital, are frequently responsible for bad outcomes. Ask: *Do any of the surgeons have mortality rates that are prompting the hospital to take any action?* An equivocal answer or "no comment" may be revealing.

A PRO has a statutory obligation to monitor care of Medicare patients. Ask PRO officials: *What actions have you taken or are you planning about this situation? Do you have either a review or a sanctions process under way against any physicians? Have you sent notice letters to any physicians? How many? At what hospitals? Has the sanction process led yet to withdrawal of any physician's Medicare participation?*

Federal laws and regulations do not permit a PRO to give out individual physician data or physicians' names. In flagrant situations, this is nonetheless information a reporter may try to get, whether from a PRO official, hospital personnel, other doctors, medical society officials, or state medical licensing boards. Some state boards regularly publish their disciplinary actions.

Even when a hospital has an apparently lower mortality rate than other hospitals, ask: *Do you credit this to superior care or the fact that this hospital primarily attracts an economically upscale, relatively healthy, paying population and few indigents and therefore has a population expected to have better-than-average outcomes?*

Were there measures the hospital took to arrive at these favorable outcomes? One community hospital, for example, upgraded its coronary intensive care unit, placed it under the charge of a highly trained cardiologist, and stood out when statistics were published.

A few cautions:

• Remember that association is not causation. There may be reasonable explanations for many unfavorably high figures.

• Remember that there is a *possible range of error* in even the most carefully collected statistics. One newspaper reported, "The specific mortality rates . . . can be used by patients as a guide. . . . For example, the typical Medicare patient with heart disease admitted to X Medical Center has a 96 percent chance of walking out alive. At Y University Medical Center, 87 of 100 such patients survived."

Anyone knowledgeable about numbers might ask, What is the range of possible error of these figures? Given the many pitfalls of gathering such statistics, any difference of a few points may be meaningless. And if the number of patients is small, even a large apparent difference may tell you nothing.

• Remember the laws of *chance* and *variability.* If you examine all 6,000 U.S. hospitals by the same methods HCFA did in March 1986, you might expect around 300 of them—5 percent—to appear to have abnormally high or low death rates by chance alone. And any one statistic is only a snapshot. A hospital's results over any one period may look more or less favorable than its results over a longer period. To see what is really happening, you need a "motion picture" that shows what happens over time, canceling out temporary runs of good or bad luck.

Does this mean the figures for even a full year may be an aberration? A year is a pretty good period, but a statistician would put far more faith in a two- or three-year look.

• We shouldn't abandon this important story after one look. Go back to the hospital, the doctors, the PRO in three or six months or a year or more and ask: *What has been done?*

Cancer Rates and Cancer "Cures"

What's a cure? Normally, it means no more evidence of disease, no recurrence, a normal life span as far as that disease is concerned. But for one disease—cancer—doctors sometimes talk of *5-year* and occasionally *10-year cure rates*. With many types of cancer, most patients, but by no means all, who survive 5 years will have no recurrence. The 10-year rate is sometimes added, and should be, to be honest, for breast cancer and prostate cancer—just two examples of cancers with many deaths after 5 or even 10 years later. The 5-year relative survival rate in 1974 (the last year for which a full 10 years' statistics were available at this writing, in late 1987) for white patients with cancer in all sites combined was 49 percent, but the rate after 10 years was 42.5. In other words, and ignoring all deaths from other causes, of every 49 cancer patients still alive in 1978 more than 6—more than 1 in every 7—had died of cancer by 1984. The 5-year relative survival rate for white females with breast cancer diagnosed in 1974 was 76.1 percent. The same group's 10-year survival was 63 percent, and the 15-year rate, were it known, would be even lower, such is breast cancer's oft-long-delayed toll.

In short, the fact that not all cancer patients will survive means no one can truly tell until years later who are cured and who are not. In plain English, a cure should mean only that the patient very certainly does not have the disease anymore. Thus, it is more accurate to report 5-year, 10-year, and even longer *survival rates,* if available, rather than "cure rates." Officials seeking to justify funds for cancer research, and many physicians who want to give patients hope, understandably like to speak of cure rates.

Doctors who treat cancer often report their 5-year survival rate *even though* not all the patients have survived for 5 years yet. This was done in 1985, for example, when oncologists—cancer doctors—at many centers reported the cumulative results of some newer treatments of breast cancer. Instead of reporting *absolute survival* alone—how many patients lived exactly how long—they used a *life table method* or *actuarial method* to say: Enough of our patients have been followed for 5 years, and enough for 1, 2, 3, or 4 years, for us to say with confidence what the 5-year survival rate for the whole group will be.

This is considered statistically honest and respectable if completely described. In fact, one statistician says, "It is wrong if it is not reported. It is the only way we can know how we are progressing in this difficult disease." But the method should be described in our news stories too, to be honest.

So should another important difference, that between absolute survival from cancer and relative survival. *Absolute survival,* or *observed survival,* is simply the actual proportion of patients still alive after X years, considering *deaths from all causes,* cancer or otherwise. *Relative survival,* the higher figure you will commonly see, is calculated by *adjusting* the observed survival to take into account the normal life expectancy of a similar population. In effect, you try to gauge the effect of cancer alone by removing the effect of all other causes of death—heart attack, auto accidents, shootings, or whatever.

Relative survival rates more accurately show progress against cancer. But they do not mean that that many people will really live that long, all causes considered. The 5-year relative survival rate was 48.7 percent for all patients diagnosed with cancer between 1977 and 1983, as reported by the federal National Cancer Institute—NCI—in 1986. The observed survival for that period was 38 percent. (Most skin cancers, which are most easily cured, are not counted in this overall rate. Melanoma is the only skin cancer included in federal or other overall cancer incidence and survival rates. Overall cancer mortality rates include other skin cancer deaths.)

Many news stories reporting cancer statistics skip mentioning relative survival altogether. The lead and headline just say something like "49% of Cancer Patients Survive." To be honest, we should say we're reporting relative survival and explain it— perhaps as "survival from cancer" or "the chance of surviving the effects of cancer"—and to convey the true picture also give the actual survival rate, considering other causes of death. No matter how you look at it—and granted that it is a necessary way to measure progress against cancer—relative survival is not real survival. More than half of all people who get cancer are already 65 and older, so it is not surprising that many die of other causes. It is also quite possible, however, that some of the deaths that have been ignored—deaths from heart disease or pneumonia, say—were influenced by patients' having been treated for cancer and left physically weakened.

If you really want to know a 10-year, not just a 5-year, survival rate for any cancer, or if you want to know the actual observed rates, you usually have to ask for these figures. Neither the NCI nor the American Cancer Society, which gets its figures from the NCI, advertises them much to the public.

You will sometimes, too, see a cancer researcher reporting patients' *mean* or *median* survival, that is, how long a group of patients have lived on the average by one of these measures. The mean does tell you how well half the patients did. But the measure picked may be the best-sounding one. And neither tells you how many people have survived how much longer or how briefly. For that you need to see a fuller explanation or a revealing table or graph.

The Important Questions about Cancer

There are three important questions about cancer today: *Is it on the increase? Is survival increasing as a result of all the new treatments? Is better treatment bringing down death rates?*

The answer to none of these questions is completely clear-cut or simple or without controversy. In all, the situation is different for each kind of cancer, and the evidence and the arguments about the evidence shift from year to year. This is not the place to try to settle them, but any reporter seeking some answers should be aware that there are controversies and should know some basic facts.

The following are the latest figures at this writing:*

• *Cancer incidence*—the overall probability of getting cancer—has been increasing by an average of 0.7 percent yearly, or by 5.4 percent in 10 years. Even eliminating the devastating effects of lung cancer, due largely to smoking, there was a 3.9 percent increase. The greatest increase took place in people over 55, but there was also a slow and steady increase—0.2 percent yearly—in younger people. Breast, colon, and prostate cancers were among those that increased; uterine cancer and leukemia declined.

• The overall 5-year *survival rate* was 48.6 percent for all patients diagnosed between 1974 and 1976, 48.7 for those diagnosed between 1977 and 1983. In short, there was little change between these periods. There were improvements for those with prostate, testis, colon and rectum, and children's cancers as well as Hodgkin's disease and other lymphomas. And the reported 5-year survival for those under 55 was 59 percent.

• The cancer *death rate*—much debated when people try to decide whether or not there has been a cancer epidemic—has increased by an average 0.5 percent yearly and by 1984 was up 4.2 percent in 10 years. Remove the effect of lung cancer, and the overall rate would have stayed about constant. For the under-55 population—79 percent of the U.S. population—the death rate did drop by 6.7 percent between 1975 and 1984. For age groups 55 and older, however, death rates increased in this period (by 1.7 percent for those aged 55 to 64 and by 8 percent for those 65 and older). The prostate cancer death rate increased. Rates fell for colon and rectal, testicular, and uterine cancers and Hodgkin's disease. Breast cancer deaths increased by about 0.2 percent a year, though declining by more than 1

---

*From the *1986 Annual Cancer Statistics Review, National Cancer Institute* (December 1986). By all means see the latest edition. Unless otherwise indicated, all references here are to overall cancer rates for all sites, ages, races, and sexes combined—and generally represent patients diagnosed for various periods between 1974 and 1984. The *Review*'s incidence and mortality (but not survival) rates are generally age-adjusted to eliminate differences in age distribution between various parts of the population.

percent a year in women under 50 until the 1986 analysis showed a 7 percent increase from 1983 to 1984. This could have been either a worrisome change or a random fluctuation — it will take longer to tell.

Are we or are we not, then, seeing more true cures as a result of all the new methods — chemotherapies and others — being used to treat cancer? Do the facts seem confusing? There is, unfortunately, no way to describe the cancer toll or to measure progress against this disease without looking very closely at many numbers and facts and weighing various interpretations.

According to one critic, Dr. John Bailar:[3]

• The most telling rate "if you want to know how we're doing" is the death rate, "the most fundamental measure of clinical outcome," and if you look at all cancer, the death rate has shown "a slow and steady increase over several decades . . . with no evidence of a recent downward trend or much overall effect. . . . In a clinical sense, we are losing the war on cancer."

• Many of the so-called increases in survival are to a large extent, at least, artifacts or delusions, created by new detection methods that are, first, "finding" many cancers so early that *apparent length of survival* only *seems* greater (this is *lead-time bias*) and, second, finding many benign or borderline lesions that in earlier years never would have been detected and counted because they never would have become problems.

According to Dr. Vincent DeVita, NCI's director:[4]

• Recent years have produced some "real advances" that will tell in future mortality statistics — and already are telling in the "encouraging" marked decline in the death rate for those under 55, despite an increase in incidence. The most recent figures measure diagnoses going back several years, and it takes at least 5 years to study newer treatments and "often another five to ten years" to see them used widely. Many doctors are still failing to give their patients optimal treatment, often by reducing drug dosages or stretching out treatments. Even so, the recent 5-year survivals of nearly 49 percent show a marked improvement over the 42 percent for those diagnosed in 1970–73 or 38 percent in 1960–63.

• Critics of current treatments also ignore great recent improvements in prolongation of life and quality of life, even when there is no ultimate cure—the many sarcoma patients retaining their limbs, for example, or the discovery that "in early breast cancer, lumpectomy and radiation [have proved] as effective as mastectomy," saving many women's breasts.

• If not only lung cancer but also all smoking-related cancers—oral cancer, bladder cancer, and others—were removed from consideration, this would indeed reveal a significant drop in the overall death rate.

To which Bailar has replied: One should also then remove from consideration the favorable effects of some declines in the death rates for various known or unknown reasons "unrelated to treatment."

The ultimate truth? We shall see. Mortality rates are fairly quick to show improvements in treatment, if any, since 60 to 65 percent of cancer deaths occur within 2 years of diagnosis. Other cancer statistics, like other health statistics the government collects, often lag years behind the current facts. This is partly because even actuarial estimates of 5-year survival rates require an adequate number of patients who have already survived for 5 years or nearly that long, partly because local and national agencies take a long time to process and analyze the figures, and partly because governments are not willing to spend much on statistics compared with spending on treatment, however crucial statistics may be to improving both treatment and prevention.

Nationwide *incidence* and *survival* statistics are collected only by the National Cancer Institute's SEER (Surveillance, Epidemiology and End Results) program. All others repeat and reinterpret only these data, unless they credit other more specific and much more limited sources. SEER currently gets its data from area-wide cancer registries in five metropolitan areas (Atlanta, Detroit, New Orleans, San Francisco–Oakland, and

Seattle), six states (Connecticut, Hawaii, Iowa, New Jersey, New Mexico, and Utah), and Puerto Rico. These cover approximately 10 percent of the U.S. population. SEER's national figures are extrapolations, unlike its cancer *mortality data,* which are actual counts of death certificates by the government's National Center for Health Statistics.

The SEER sample has existed in much of its present broadened form only since 1973. This means that all national comparisons with pre-1973 incidence and survival are suspect. A former SEER official says, "There are good reasons for believing that substantial sub-sets of SEER and pre-SEER cancer incidence data are comparable." But some may not be, and, he adds, even current SEER figures may not be "a good representation" for blacks, especially rural southern blacks.[5]

So far we have mainly discussed overall cancer progress— rates for all sites, ages, races, and sexes combined. These overall figures are meaningless if you want to know what has been happening in a particular cancer—and what has been happening in white males, white females, black males, black females, Hispanic males, Hispanic females, and so on, where the picture varies hugely. Blacks generally have higher incidence and mortality rates than whites and also poorer survival rates—and black men more so than black women.

Cancer, we have seen, also varies greatly by age, and most of the increase in chances of dying from cancer has occurred in the population over 65. (It is also true that more older people die of cancer because the risk of dying from some other causes has been reduced. But that is not a factor here because the figures have been age-adjusted for comparisons unbiased by the effect of aging alone.) There may be several possible reasons for the variations in age groups: people diagnosed at an earlier age may now be living longer to show up in the over-65 rate; there may be improved diagnosis and more-accurate reporting on death certificates; and there may be a real increase in the death rate because of other causes.

To a reporter looking at cancer, the lesson seems to be this: look at incidence, survival, *and* mortality statistics. Look at them for various groups. Then talk them over with more than one official, authority, or critic. Get more than one point of view.

A few other points about cancer:

• No incidence or mortality figures tell us much about what to expect in the future. The lung cancer epidemic was unanticipated when men, and later women, began heavy cigarette smoking in the 1920s and 1930s. Some scientists fear sharp increases in cancer in future years, perhaps the 1990s, because of today's ever-increasing exposure to what one scientist calls the "rich mix" of chemicals and chemical fumes that Americans now inhale and imbibe.

Epidemiologists are largely stumped when it comes to gauging the unknown combined effects of many factors, including many untested chemicals and other influences. (One set of synergistic chemical effects has been plainly identified: Cigarette smoking increases the chance of cancer among those exposed to asbestos, those exposed to radiation, and those using birth control pills.) Many authorities say that waiting for proof before indicting some suspect causes may be a wait for a statistical Godot who never arrives.

Critics of that point of view say that if we were to have seen a major cancer epidemic because of chemical exposures, we should have seen it already, since the huge and steady increase in exposure to industrial chemicals began 50 years ago, not yesterday.

• For now, there may have been exaggerated, though by no means unwarranted, fears of cancer epidemics caused by environmental and industrial pollution. Except for smoking and lung cancer, environmental carcinogens — potential cancer-causing chemicals in pesticides, fish, cattle feed — have had far more news coverage than any other aspect relating to cancer.

In part, this general American mind-set may have started with scientists' startling estimates some years ago that as many as 70 to 90 percent of all cancers might be related to—not necessarily solely caused by—environmental factors. Many people took the word "environmental" to mean pollution. It would have been more accurate to say "life-style" or "behavioral" *and* environmental factors, since by various recent and reasonably credible estimates, use of tobacco is probably associated with 25 to 30 percent of all cancers; alcohol consumption, 3 to 5 percent; diet (overconsumption of fats, for example), 30 to 60 percent; reproductive and sexual behavior, 7 percent; radiation (mainly natural but including medical radiation), 3 percent; food additives, perhaps 1 percent; man-made environmental (mainly chemical) pollution, 1 to 5 percent; and job exposures, 2 to 8 percent, with most estimates running 4 to 6 percent.

There is obviously much uncertainty and overlap. And this is not to say that association means sole cause, that dietary habits alone, for one example, cause 30 to 60 percent of all cancers. Diet may more likely be one of several *risk factors* interacting to do so.

On the subject of chemicals, Dr. Bruce Ames—inventor of the Ames test for mutagens (mutation-causing, hence possibly birth-defect-causing agents) and carcinogens—has argued, "It is not sensible to try to regulate very low levels of man-made carcinogens" or to "chase after smaller and smaller amounts of the next carcinogen that reaches the public eye. . . . My own estimate is that we are eating 10,000 times more of nature's pesticides—natural toxic materials made in large amount by plants to keep off insects and other predators—than we are of man-made pesticide residues. . . . Nature's pesticides are teeming with mutagens, carcinogens, and teratogens [birth-defect producers]. Cooking our food also generates mutagens and carcinogens, as all browned and burned material contains them."[6]

Other scientists strenuously disagree. They argue that we may have largely accommodated to Dr. Ames' natural carcinogens since we evolved with exposure to low-level natural or "background" x-radiation, ultraviolet light, plant carcinogens, and other natural toxins and developed the capacity to detoxify many of them and repair most spontaneous lesions. Even if this process is imperfect, it is argued, there is no reason to add any man-made burden, particularly from something so little needed as a food dye. And even "small" added burdens may cause or help trigger large numbers of cases; there are in fact many increases in cancer rates (in the general population or specific groups) in which man-made carcinogens have either been found guilty or are highly suspect.

Certainly we reporters should remember to convert some barren cancer rates or percentages into numbers. If "only" 5 percent of all new cancer cases are related to industrial exposure, this still becomes what has been called "a major public health problem resulting in 20,000 excess cancer deaths each year."[7] Ames himself has added that "we know very little" about these matters, that there have been "large increases in the use of synthetic chemicals, either for workers . . . or for all of us exposed to food additives and pesticides," and that "the key task is to determine which of the many natural and man-made carcinogenic factors we are exposed to represent major hazards and to establish practical tolerance levels."

• Full knowledge of cancer's causes and "related factors" will remain elusive for a long time. There are only a small number of ways to learn whether or not something may cause cancer: (1) often unsatisfactory surveys of human illness (which can never be real experiments in which you would "give" cancer to "human guinea pigs") and human population statistics, (2) studies in animals, in which large doses must be given to produce any results over practical lengths of time, (3) laboratory bioassays, or tests of the effects of possible cancer-causing agents on living cells or bacteria, and (4) laboratory tests for chromosome aberrations in high-risk populations like industrial workers or homeowners exposed to toxic wastes (these tests are currently proving useful). Still, all these methods are less than perfect, and some are highly imperfect. To say this, however, is not to say they may not be of help. It is not true, for example, that everything causes cancer in animals in large enough doses. Most chemicals do not.

• A final warning. Small-scale cancer incidence figures are often deceptive. A town or county may report a startling number of cases of cancer of the such and such in the area of a chemical plant or toxic waste dump. If you investigate, you may find that many U.S. census tracts or municipalities have equally large numbers just by chance and the laws of statistical variation. The same applies to that commonly reported phenomenon the *cancer cluster,* an alarming-sounding concentration of some kind of cancer in a city block or neighborhood. Most such alleged clusters turn out to be real enough, but in most cases their cause, if any, remains unresolved. Many — some authorities say almost all — are probably the result of statistical variation, in other words, chance. Only in a few cases is some reasonable possible cause, like an industrial or environmental "hot spot," identified. The difficulty for epidemiologists and reporters alike is distinguishing these real problem areas from those that only seem to exist. It takes a large number of new "problem cases" to show up against the normal cancer caseload, and it may take 5 to 40 years' exposure for true problem cases to show up at all (less for some leukemias).

Shifts, Drifts, and Blips

A death blamed on senility in 1900 would probably have been put down as "general arteriosclerosis" in 1960 and would be blamed now either on cerebrovascular disease (including strokes) or Alzheimer's disease, which has only in recent years been recognized as a cause of a large proportion of senility and death.

Medical knowledge, medical definitions, doctors' skills, doctors' diagnostic enthusiasms, and the way statisticians code disease all change. Some diseases — the connective tissue disorder called lupus and probably cancer of the pancreas — appear to have increased dramatically simply because they are being found more often. Death certificates have been called notoriously inaccurate. The number of autopsies, the most accurate method of identifying cause of death, has dropped sharply in recent years. Doctors vastly underreport problems they are legally required to report, including sexually related diseases.

These are only a few of the rocks and shoals in determining who died of what and who has what. There are also unexplained or incompletely explained drifts in the statistics, like the declines in heart disease and stomach cancer deaths. The media also affect disease rates. "I can write about toxic shock syndrome, and cases will get reported to the Minnesota Health Department," Lewis Cope of the Minneapolis *Star Tribune* reports. "I wrote about Lyme disease [a form of arthritis], and sure enough, cases flooded into health officials the next week." Then there is the "Betty Ford blip" in breast cancer incidence: a dramatic rise in discovery of new cases for a few years after that First Lady's 1974 breast cancer surgery (and a lot of coincidental publicity that year about breast cancer detection and surgery).

The Statistics of Environment and Risk

8

The public has become used to conflicting opinion. . . . Many have come to feel that for every Ph.D., there is an equal and opposite Ph.D.

— Tim Hammonds, *Food Marketing Institute*

I'd like to meet a one-handed scientist.

— Contemporary folk saying,
often heard in Washington

$\mathbf{A}$N oil spill covers beaches with black sludge and bodies of birds. The core of a nuclear power plant goes out of control, and unskilled operators do the wrong things. A community, puzzled over some strange illnesses, discovers it is sitting on a toxic waste dump.

Many of these events do not injure large numbers of people, as far as we can tell. Yet thousands are scared or concerned. There are TV news specials and newspaper headlines. And the media are typically accused of overstating, needlessly alarming, emphasizing the worst possible case, reporting half-baked and unsupported conclusions, or falsely reassuring.

We do them all sometimes. Trying to be objective, perhaps stung by such criticism, we too often write only "on the one hand, on the other hand" stories—I like to call them "he said, she said" stories—without expending any great effort to find the most-credible evidence, the most-reliable statistics, the best-informed, least-prejudiced views, the greatest probabilities.

Our problem — and the subject of this chapter — is to learn to function in situations in which the following prevail:

• Uncertainty reigns, and data are incomplete, inadequate, or nonexistent.

• We are told different things by different people, and distinguished scientists make opposing, even warring, assertions, such as "The hazard is horrendous" and "The hazard is minimal or nonexistent."

• Much of the public doesn't worry greatly about driving, using seat belts, drinking, or smoking, but it often vibrates about the often lesser and less certain dangers of nuclear power and chemicals in our foods. Someone said, "Americans want to be protected from nuclear accidents so they can go hang gliding."

The public is not entirely illogical. It is easier to cope with the known than the unknown and mysteriously threatening. We decide for ourselves whether to accept the risks of driving, drinking, smoking, or hang gliding. We may feel very different about a risk someone imposes on us — or a risk that could decimate a population if the worst happens.

We have been told too often that such and such is safe, only to learn later that the assurance was wrong or that new data changed the picture. Fish and birds have died or dwindled away, waterways have been polluted, men and women have been fatally exposed in the workplace. There are toxic waste dumps. There is acid rain. There have been nuclear accidents. There was Chernobyl. There are some 60,000 chemicals on the market, and only a small number have been adequately tested. In the words of Dr. Peter Montague of Princeton University, "All human systems are growing." The problems will become greater, not less.

What should we tell readers, listeners, and editors when they ask, Why don't "they" know? Why can't they give us some answers right away?

Scientists grappling with these questions ask us to understand, and explain, half a dozen basic facts.*

(1) *The true complexity of the problem.* Almost every environmental or chemical effect on people or their surroundings involves many interactions between many factors, often at many times and many places.

Take the relationship between pollution and cancer. What kinds of pollution are we talking about? What kinds of cancer? Are there interactions between causes? Are there multiple causes? Who are exposed? Are they equally vulnerable? Do they also smoke or drink a lot or have exposures to other carcinogens? Are there other possible explanations, that is, confounding variables or biases? Are the numbers large enough to be reliable? Are there enough cases to show up in a population of millions, and how can we distinguish them from other cancers? Since cancer often has a long latency period, will we have to wait 20 or 30 years to find out?

The greenhouse effect (carbon dioxide buildup and the resulting warming of the atmosphere caused by our burning fossil fuels) and the effects of acid rain, of fluorocarbons on the ozone layer, and of nuclear waste disposal will take decades to assess. In many cases—radiation at Hiroshima, Agent Orange and dioxin in Vietnam—exposures are unknown. In most cases, true human trials (controlled exposure of human subjects to some pollutant) are ethically impossible.

The upshot: several layers of constraints and uncertainties, each worsened by the one before. Often no one knows what all the pieces of information should be. Little wonder that there is rarely overwhelming evidence for or against a direct cause and

---

*In this chapter I drew substantially on the presentations and often the words of Dr. Michael Greenberg, professor of urban studies and director, Public Policy and Education, Hazardous and Toxic Substances Research Center, Rutgers University, and Dr. Peter Montague, director, Hazardous Waste Research Program, Princeton University, at symposiums sponsored by the Council for the Advancement of Science Writing. Cass Peterson of the *Washington Post* and others added to the questions reporters may ask.

effect, not to mention any way of easy prediction or quick solution.

As the Conservation Foundation has put it, "When the weather forecaster is vague about how much it will snow tomorrow, if at all, how can we expect scientists to calculate how many degrees the earth will warm up in 40 years because of carbon dioxide loading?"[1]

(2) *The limitations of science.* Since human beings are not laboratory rats, and controlled human experiments are out of the question, environmental scientists must rely on many *quasi-experimental designs,* something less than true controlled trials. Examples: comparisons with historical data (often deceptive), case-control studies (comparisons of affected people with a similar, one hopes, unaffected group), descriptive or observational studies (just looking at and describing something, without comparisons), and animal studies (which may or may not apply to humans). Many of these are weak in pinpointing cause and effect, and none is definitive, so their conclusions can vary sharply.

The measurements themselves are often difficult, and often discouragingly expensive. "Acute diseases are fairly easy to measure," one environmental scientist says. "But chronic diseases — say, nervous system effects or effects on the fetus — are devilishly hard to recognize with precision, and they may take 20 years to show up. So we use a looser and looser screen and end up with many false positives."[2]

Because methods of evaluation (mathematical models and the like) also differ, different scientists may come to different conclusions when they look at the same data. Moreover, all scientists are not equal, and opportunities for good research are not always present or funded, so studies are often of poor quality. The effects of the toxic waste dump at Love Canal have remained controversial because of hasty, incomplete research.

A National Center for Health Statistics study group concerned with environment-related health effects scrutinized 50 studies purporting to measure health hazards and their outcomes. It found only 4 that directly related exposure and out-come data, and even in those the methods were weak.[3]

(3) *The limitations of the best data.* The data may have been carefully collected after all. The statistical tests may produce a comforting *P value* of < .05, or less than a 5 percent chance that the relationship could have occurred by chance. But that is still only a *probability.* It could be an *artifact,* caused by unknown confounders. And in 1 such study in 20, on the average — so say the laws of probability — chance will produce a misleading re-sult. "Actually," one scientist says, "estimates of risk usually have wide confidence limits, and the majority are really guesstimates. More often than not, the best we can do is guess at the order of magnitude within which the risk falls."[4]

As part of the same effect, *science cannot prove a negative.* Com-pletely aside from the practical difficulty of finding small effects that take years to show up — and the impossibility of ever being sure you haven't missed something — no study can ever prove that something is not harmful or does not exist. As one statisti-cian explains, probability "practically guarantees that a small number of studies will show some *'statistically significant'* findings if enough studies are carried out. As a result, we can never be 100 percent sure that the null hypothesis of no association . . . is true."[5]

One more mathematical fact. You may study a satisfyingly large sample or population and find some remarkable effects, real deviations from the norm, at both ends of your distribution or scale — at both extremes if you've drawn a curve. But they may not be abnormal. Such results are actually *expected* because of the *large-sample effect,* which says there are usually striking extremes at both *tails* of a distribution.

In the same way, disease rates may show some sharp varia-tions when you compare the census figures for two census tracts or localities. These too may be *natural variations,* not necessarily aberrations.

(4) *The limitations of analysis.* Looking at the results of a

study — almost always the results in a *sample,* since few studies cover everybody in a population — a scientist must try to extrapolate or project or infer to a larger or another population. For instance, he must try to extrapolate the effects of a high dose of a substance or a physical effect like radiation to someone who gets a low dose.

To do so accurately, he needs to ask: Am I dealing with a *linear relationship* — one in which a dose of 0.01, say, has a ten-thousandth of the effect of a dose of 100 (on a graph, a straight line ascending from bottom left to upper right as the dose increases)? Or is this a *nonlinear relationship* in which there is a *threshold* at some point, below which low doses have no effect and are safe?

Some relationships in nature are indeed linear, and even more are linear only in part or definitely nonlinear. But a scientist pondering the effects of radiation or the fumes of some chemical does not know which relationship applies and has no way of finding out. What he usually has in hand are data from exposures to high doses in humans or animals or both. Asked to help make a practical decision on whether low doses are safe or dangerous, he often must make a *policy* or *value judgment,* not a mathematical decision.

He can decide that there is no threshold and there must indeed be a linear *dose-response effect.* This decision is probably on the safe side: it should protect everyone, but it may also shut down a plant if low doses can't be avoided. Or he can assume that the relationship is nonlinear and that low doses are probably safe. Those exposed may be at some risk; the plant stays open.

The problem is more complicated, of course. There are nonlinear dose-response relationships in which there may be no effect at a very low dose, then a sudden rise at a dose not much greater. Pity the analyst — or the unsuspecting exposed.

The above is a problem in *model analysis.* Using the wrong statistical *model* — wrongly assuming a linear relationship or wrongly assuming that other types of data are normally distributed in a typical bell-shaped curve (see "Variability" in Chapter 3)—is called *model misspecification.*

To avoid it, statisticians often use what they call *nonparametric methods* to look at their data. These are methods that don't let a few very large or very small or very wild numbers run away with the analysis. Example: using just plus or minus signs rather than specific counts for reactions to a substance or a medical treatment. You count up and compare the number of pluses and minuses. Or you might group your counts by rank from least to greatest. These methods can sometimes be valuable. Or—remember, nothing's simple—they can sometimes be used to "prove" something that doesn't look proved to anyone else.

Environmental analysts must also deal with problems in *scaling* or *scale analysis,* usually how to *scale up* from a sample to a larger universe. Inappropriate scaling can produce two common errors made by both journalists and analysts:

• You see 2 or 3 or 20 cases of a disease and assume the results apply to a larger population. This is the *individualistic fallacy.* Your sample must be large enough and representative enough before you may reliably and validly extrapolate.

A kind of cousin is the *healthy-worker effect,* in which you look at the workers exposed to substance A, find they are actually healthier than the general population, and exonerate the substance—possibly wrongly. The workers are probably not representative of the general population, because those who get jobs are normally healthier. They should be compared with their peers, say workers in another industry or another department.

• You study 10 cities along the Ohio River and find a relationship between water quality and reported bladder cancer. You assume there is probably a cause-and-effect relationship, that the same is probably true anyplace with the same water quality, and individuals or groups of individuals in other cities with similar water quality must be victims of the same problem. You may be engaging in the *ecological fallacy.* If you studied 100 towns with the same kind of water or did a careful comparison of bladder cancer patients with comparable controls, you might find that something entirely different caused the cancers. Be wary of accepting either individual or ecological data alone.

(5) *The limitations of risk assessment.* In the 1970s, *risk assessment* and *risk analysis* became Washington buzz words. Risk assessment is both an "in" way and often a necessary way of using an amalgam—a grab bag—of studies and facts and conjectures to try to make a practical assessment of risk, whether the risk of PCBs (polychlorinated biphenyls) or the dye Red No. 3 or not installing air bags in our cars.

Risk assessment is often escalated into *risk-benefit assessment*—considering and weighing both the probable bad and the probable good. In 1981 President Reagan issued a highly controversial executive order permitting regulatory action (unless ordered by Congress) only if "the potential benefits to society . . . outweigh the potential costs to society."

Both risk assessment and, emphatically, risk-benefit assessment involve stacks of unknowns, including all the pitfalls we have already discussed. Former Environmental Protection Administrator William D. Ruckelshaus has said, "Risk assessment data can be like the tortured spy. If you torture it long enough, it will tell you anything you want to know."[6] Or anything you want to tell people.

The process is only in part a matter of science. It involves psychology, culture, ideology, economics, and politics. Even the scientific considerations, like the risk of a substance X, are often unquantifiable, let alone the nonscientific ones. It is much easier to assess the risk to groups than to individuals. It is easier to assess a risk today than the risk 20 to 40 years down the line. It took that long for the effects of cigarette smoking to become a clear-cut epidemic.

At its best, however, risk assessment gets all the facts and uncertainties out on the table for public consideration. "We must assume that life now takes place in a minefield of risks from hundreds, perhaps thousands, of substances," Ruckelshaus also has said. "No more can we tell the public: 'You are home free with an adequate margin of safety.' . . . If the government gets better at both assessing and managing risk, and we do it accurately, people will have a better sense of the risks and will act sensibly."

What officials, and the media, too often fail to convey about most present risk assessment is its uncertainty. Some of this uncertainty may be forever inevitable, but much need not be. Frederick Mosteller says,

One reason the science is so weak in risk assessments is that although billions may be spent on the programs—cleaning the air or water—and millions arguing about the feeble studies that are available, practically nothing is spent for the research needed to get some sensible understanding. Most of these big problems go on for decades, and research not started now won't be completed when needed later. I have just reviewed three of these big decisions, where everyone explained to everyone how poor the data were and how arbitrary the decisions. They keep looking at lousy data and acting as if no one could do better. We badly need substantial research programs lasting several years to sort matters out.

(6) *The limitations of the scientists.* Scientists are noble and ignoble, unbiased and biased, honest and dishonest—better than average, I think, in all these respects, but still just people. There is some dishonesty, we have learned, even in the peer-reviewed world of scientific publication. And there is the far vaster world of modern communication with far lower standards in which scientists of varying quality are also heard.

Given the emotions surrounding risk and the environment, even the best scientists with the best motives can be gripped by biases, prejudices, political beliefs, and judgments based on different training and values—also, at times, their personal economic interests.

"The technical community has developed increasingly sophisticated public relations techniques," Dr. Dorothy Nelkin observes. "Most risk-oriented public relations efforts are generated by industries involved in controversial, science-based technologies," which develop "palatable synonyms" like "nuclear parks" instead of "nuclear power plants." Environmental groups use public relations and convinced scientists too, ranging in objectivity from the conscientious to the tendentious. The chief culprits on all sides—industry, government, environmental groups—are scientists who "make sweeping judgments on the basis of incomplete, and hence inadequate, data," emphasize their own views, and suppress or minimize conflicting evidence, a Twentieth Century Fund task force concluded.[7]

Tufts University's Drs. Jean Mayer and Jeanne Goldberg write, for example, of the food supply: "All too often the Bermuda Triangle of consumers, industry and regulatory agencies will not cooperate together to promote safety. . . . Time and time again, industry takes the defensive, trying to protect its 'turf' when it should strive for the public interest. Consumer groups tend to leap to conclusions with the hysteria of someone shouting 'fire!' in a crowded theater."[8]

Who's Believable?

How can we decide who or what is most credible? The most believable results will have many, but not necessarily all, of seven characteristics:

(1) *They have been successfully repeated*—scientists say *replicated*—with much the same results in at least most of several different studies in different places in different populations at different times. There should also be supporting data from animal and laboratory experiments.

(2) *They have been successfully tested by more than one method.* This means both *reevaluation* of the data by different mathematical techniques—common in institutions where the science is careful—and a check on the result by different kinds of studies or analyses. A valid result should be *method-independent.* "You should still find the result," says Rutgers' Greenberg, "even when you try to 'destroy' it."

(3) _They score high for statistical significance,_ with only a small probability that the same result could have been found by chance.

(4) _They are statistically strong._ The greater the odds of an effect, the greater the _strength_ of an association. If exposure to substance A seems to make your chance of getting cancer 1.5 times as likely, that translates as an astounding-sounding 50 percent excess risk. But given all the limitations of human data, it may or may not be a real risk. As we said earlier, if the risk is 10 times as likely — the relative risk of lung cancer in cigarette smokers compared with nonsmokers — the odds are pretty good that something is happening.

(5) _They are specific._ Substance A causes disease B. This is a more specific association than a sweeping statement that substance A may cause everything from hair loss to cancer to ingrown toenails. Some causes do indeed have multiple effects, but it takes more than sweeping statements to establish this.

Also, what specifically is to blame for a problem? A study indicates that drinking water is causing cancer. Is it groundwater or river water? Is the accusation based on a chemical analysis of the water? Or suspended solids? Or specific toxic substances?

(6) _The results cannot be explained by other relationships or confounding factors:_ the healthy-worker effect or cigarette smoking or population migration or failure to stratify — that is, to break down the data by age, sex, income, race, occupation, and so on.

(7) _The data and its possible weaknesses are described in detail._ How sure or unsure are you that the data are reliable, valid, statistically sound? Is there such a discussion? "There is never enough data," Greenberg says. "There is always a lot of missing data. There are always missing variables. I tend to have more belief in the individual who admits data weaknesses."

Questions to Ask

Many of the possible questions in Chapter 5 also apply here. But let's repeat several in slightly different form and add a few more. Some apply in most situations, some in specific ones.

What is your evidence? What do you base your conclusions on?

Have you done a study? Has it been published or (at least) *accepted by a recognized journal?*

What type of study did you do? What was the experimental design? Did you work with an epidemiologist on the design? See Chapter 4 for kinds of studies and their uses and worth. Studies range from mere collections of anecdotes (worth little except as leads for more research) to more systematic observations of cases (important but usually not adequate to establish cause and effect) to more rigorous studies or experiments with proper scientific procedures and, if possible, controls.

May I read a copy? Read the full paper or article. You may find some surprises.

What are your data? What are your numbers?

When you are told about "rates" and "excess risks": *What are the actual figures? How many people are affected out of how large a population?*

What sort of rates would you expect normally? What are the rates elsewhere? How do you know?

Are your assumptions based on human or animal data? If animal data, see page 72. If human data: *How many people have you looked at? Are your study groups large enough to give you confidence that your conclusions are correct?*

Do you believe your sample—the people studied—*is representative of the general population? Or of the population you're trying to apply it to?*

How did you pick your sample—at random?

Or if conclusions are based on cases, victims supposedly affected by some agent: *Have you yourself observed the effects in the people you're talking about, or did you have to depend on retrospective recall?* A neighborhood discovers it rests on a toxic waste dump, and people say, "That's why I've been sick!" A human enough reaction, sometimes right, often wrong.

Did you examine them? Who made the diagnoses? Were the diagnoses firm?

Was everyone who was exposed affected? Do you have any information or figures on their exposures?

Could the association or result have occurred just by chance? Exactly what are your figures for statistical significance—the probability or confidence that chance did not rule, as expressed in a *P value* or *confidence level* and in *confidence limits*. (See "Probability" in Chapter 2.)

Have you worked with a biostatistician?

Are you comparing the right figures? Perhaps you can think of a more diplomatic way to get at this. But Dr. Thomas Vogt gives some striking examples "from real data . . . similar to conclusions reached every day by [scientific] authors and readers who select the wrong statistics to prove a point":[9]

• Someone reported that the *proportional mortality* due to congenital malformations in babies dying before age one was 14 percent in 1960—that is, of all babies who died, 14 percent died of congenital malformations—compared with only 6 percent in 1920. Startling? No. The infant *death rate*—or risk of dying—from congenital malformations was 5.1 per 1,000 births in 1920 but only 3.6 per 1,000 births in 1960 (14 percent of the 1960 infant death rate of only 26 deaths per 1,000 compared with 6 percent of the huge 1920 infant death rate of 85.8 per 1,000). Other causes of death had declined, giving malformations a larger proportion of a smaller total.

• Someone said widows constituted 15 percent but widowers only 5 percent of the 400 suicides in a California county from 1961 to 1965, "suggesting that males better tolerate the loss of their marital partners." Census data—not included in the state medical journal article—showed that there were five times as many widows as widowers, and the suicide *rate* among widows (rather than the *proportion* of all suicides) was actually only 4 per 1,000, compared with 6 per 1,000 among widowers.

The message to reporters: stop, read, listen, and question.

What is really known and what is still unknown? What is the degree of uncertainty? Are you missing any data you would like to have had?

What possible biases or weaknesses or qualifications still apply to your findings or conclusion? Are you concerned about possible biases or confounding factors? Could anything else — any other variables — have accounted for your results?

What evidence might have led you to a different conclusion?

Most scientists will give good marks to a clear, forthright statement on such matters, unless the defects are overwhelming.

Are you concluding that there is a cause-and-effect relationship? Or only a possibly suspicious association? Or a mere statistical association?

Have you found a dose-response relationship? Do you have information or estimates on dose-response ratios — how much of this substance causes how much harm? Or is the answer "We don't know"?

Can you draw a dose-response curve or only a possible one? Are you assuming there is an effect at a low dose because you believe there is a linear relationship — and no threshold or cutoff — between low and known high doses? Or is there some other reason for your extrapolation?

Do most people in your field agree that this relationship is right for this agent?

If there is a possible cause-and-effect relationship or a highly suspicious association: *To whom in the population does the risk apply? What's the extent of the risk? Can you say what it means to individuals?*

Is the risk a definite number or rate, or is there a range of possibilities, depending on your assumptions or different interpretations of your data?

Is the risk given for the current exposure level or for some proposed, projected, or feared level?

What's the highest safe level we can tolerate? Or is the only safe level zero? With cancer-causing compounds, the federal government (by law) generally assumes that there is no safe level or threshold and that any quantity poses some risk. As the law has been interpreted, however—and sometimes controversially interpreted—some compounds known to be carcinogenic have been permitted for use at levels believed to pose a *de minimus* risk, a risk so small it is considered negligible. As a rule of thumb, a one-in-a-million entire-lifetime risk of cancer has been considered *de minimus*.

Might we be exposed to multiple risks or cumulative effects? Are there individual sensitivities?

What is the relative importance of this risk compared with others that we face in daily life?

Are there alternatives to this agent, and what do we know about their risks?

In reporting on radiation—from a Three Mile Island or Chernobyl—reporters often fail to differentiate between actual human exposure—that is, how much of the radioactivity has reached or can be expected to affect people—and radioactive fallout in the air, water, soil, crops, and milk. Ask: *What are the fallout levels in the air, water, and soil? How much has reached or may reach food supplies? What is the current or expected whole-body exposure? How much is a lethal dose*—one causing imminent death? *How much is a harmful dose?* From the standpoint of cancer? Of future birth defects? Of early death?

How do the radiation levels compare with the area's natural background—the radioactivity always present in air, water, soil, and rocks? A comparison with background levels may sometimes reveal almost no added increment. But be aware that, in one environmentalist's words, "this is a time-honored way to minimize adverse effects."

Example: A Soviet report on the Chernobyl nuclear power plant disaster said that fatalities in the European Soviet Union would be less than 0.05 percent of the death rate due to spontaneously arising cancer (whether from background radioactivity or other causes), that deaths from thyroid cancer would be an added 1 percent of the expected number, and that deaths caused by contaminated food supplies "may result in an additional death rate . . . that does not exceed .4 percent" of the normal cancer death rate. After studying radiation tables and normal cancer death rates in the Chernobyl reactor's vicinity, U.S. authorities calculated that the Soviets might be facing between 5,000 and 40,000 added deaths and perhaps twice as many nonlethal cancers. (The estimate depends on the authority. An estimate from one U.S. government task force: up to 10,320 cancer deaths over 70 years. Worldwide, according to many estimates, there could be up to 75,000 added deaths, with a midrange estimate of 39,000.)[10]

Cass Peterson of the *Washington Post* says,

Environmental reporters seldom see epidemiological studies, like those you've been describing. Such studies are rare in the cases of the environmental hazards we have to cover—a chemical brew leaking from a toxic waste dump, or pesticide or drug contamination in the food supply. Regulators and health officials generally have to rely on animal studies. Federal law requires a battery of such studies before a new pesticide or chemical can be marketed in this country. Many older pesticides and chemical compounds were put on the market before these laws were passed, however, so there's often what regulators call a *data gap*—missing information on toxicity or environmental impact.

Ask: *What animal studies have been done on this chemical's or pesticide's chronic health effects? Were they long-term studies* (such as two-year or longer bioassays for cancer) *or short-term* (six-month or so) *feeding studies?* Short-term studies yield quick results but are not as good as long-term studies. *Were studies conducted for mutagenicity and reproductive effects as well as cancer?*

How many species were tested? Usually it's mice and rats, but often dogs and monkeys are used as well.

What was the method of exposure? Inhalation? Feeding? Skin exposure (dermal)? Something in our food supply might best be tested by a feeding study; a workplace exposure, by skin exposure or inhalation. *Was more than one method of exposure tested?*

Have the results been reviewed by outside scientists? The Environmental Protection Agency (EPA) has scientific advisory panels to do this.

What are the data gaps? Since there may be only a single study or none at all for some older substances, we should tell readers what isn't known.

And specifically for pesticides: *Has a federal tolerance or maximum permitted residue been set for this product? What foods does it cover? What information was used to set the tolerance? Has use increased since the tolerance was set?* Is the tolerance still adequate? *Are there recent studies of actual residues in foods?*

Some more general — and some personal — questions are often useful.

Do your data support a decision to ban or regulate a substance or activity? Are you basing your warning of hazard — or assurance of safety — on studies or data or on historical experience of a similar kind? That is, Are you making a *projection,* a statement of what will happen, based on the past record, if things don't change, or a *prediction,* a statement of what you think will happen? *Is your projection or prediction based on your own judgment, fears, or hopes?*

How much — we cannot repeat this too often — *is certain? Uncertain?*

A question that you might pose in your own mind rather than ask aloud: *Are you making a scientific assertion or a nonscientific one?* Author Rodger Pirnie Doyle writes, "There is nothing intrinsically wrong with making a judgment on the basis of extrascientific considerations, but it is important to distinguish between this kind . . . and that based strictly on the scientific evidence."[11] Harvard's Dr. Harvey Fineberg says, "In reporting controversy, the first thing a reporter ought to be able to do is distinguish a scientific from a nonscientific assertion." But, he adds, "All truth is not science" — unproved does not always mean untrue.

What do other people think? Are there other studies or conclusions that bear out what you say? Can you cite specific ones I can look up? Any report in a good journal, or sponsored by any organization with scientific pretensions, should list these as references.

Who has reviewed your data and your report? Has there been peer or quality review — by reviewers or editors for a journal or by a review committee for some agency or organization?

Are your data and analyses open to public scrutiny?

What do your critics say? Who are they? Who else, on either side of the question, can I talk to? (And a reporter might ask these other parties: *Have I asked the right questions?*)

Is there any common ground between you and those who disagree? Do you agree on any of the facts? Or even on the premises or issues or questions involved?

Some scientists have their own, strongly felt political, social, or economic connections, and they might not reveal them to you unless you ask. This does not mean their work or assertions should not be judged on their own merits. Almost everyone is connected to something and has opinions and prejudices. In the words of Dr. Gary Friedman, "Ultimately we must all rely on the integrity and objectivity of the researcher and the basic scientific process of repetition of studies by other investigators."[12]

So, judge research on its merits. Still, you may often want to ask: *What are your personal values on this subject? Your politics? Have you taken similar positions before or sometimes disagreed? Do you belong to any organizations or groups that have taken similar positions?*

Who — what government agency or agencies or companies or just who — *is supporting your work? Who has supported it in the past to any significant extent?*

If questioning a member of a political administration who is stating some conclusion or policy, ask or find out: *What is the administration's policy on this? Is your conclusion the same as the adminis-*

tration's? Have people outside the government come to the same conclusion?

We need to remember that opinions, connections, and sources of financing are not necessarily indictments. But, given the topic, the public may have a right to know them. And there are prejudice peddlers.

If you run into resistance, you may want to mention that the *New England Journal of Medicine* now requires all its contributors to disclose any pertinent commercial, institutional, financial, or funding connections. These are the journal's instructions to authors:

The journal expects authors to disclose any commercial associations that might pose a conflict of interest in connection with the submitted article. All funding sources supporting the work should be routinely acknowledged in a footnote, as should all institutional or corporate affiliations of the authors. Other kinds of associations, such as consultancies, stock ownership or other equity interests or patent licensing arrangements, should be disclosed to the editor in a covering letter at the time of submission.

This information is held in confidence while the article is under review, and "if the manuscript is accepted the editor will discuss with the authors how best to disclose the relevant information."

Also, examine your own opinions and biases. When reporting the news, set them aside.

Evaluating Environmental Hazards

Princeton's Dr. Peter Montague and others add some more detailed suggestions and questions to help evaluate environmental and chemical hazards. (The language in this section is in largest part, but not entirely, Montague's.)

In comparing hazards to their *natural background levels*—important to do whenever possible—remember that these are not necessarily safe. Background radiation and natural toxins in food can affect humans and cause cancer. But they are usually the least hazardous we can expect to achieve.

How big is a big hazard? As a rule of thumb (not always true but a good guideline to decide whether something deserves serious investigation), a 10 percent increase above background is something to pay attention to. A factor-of-2 increase (a doubling) should be of real concern. A factor-of-10 increase is big; a factor-of-100 increase, very big.

If there is no natural background level, look for *federal or state standards* for workers. It is common to assume that the general public will be adequately protected by a contamination level 10 to 100 times lower than that permitted in the workplace. The public also, of course, includes infants, elderly, chronically ill, urbanites who breathe a mixture of many contaminants, and many people who are more sensitive than others. Thus the reasoning that the public will be protected by a standard 10 to 100 times tighter than a workplace standard has its limits but is probably sound as a general rule in the absence of information to the contrary.

You can also find a federal or state standard for water or air. Ask: *Are there drinking water or air standards? Is there an OSHA* (Occupational Safety and Health Administration) *standard for this chemical?*

Given such a standard, you can calculate how much water or air would be needed to dilute a substance to acceptable standards. A company was dumping only 10 gallons of trichloroethylene onto the ground a year—"really no problem," the company said, though it reached the groundwater. The federal *criterion* (the EPA distinguishes between a merely suggested *criterion* and a legally enforceable *standard*) for this chemical is 2.7 ppb—parts per billion, or micrograms per liter. It would take more than 3.5 billion gallons of water to dilute 10 gallons to this level; at an average per capita fluid consumption of two quarts a day, 3.5 billion gallons is enough drinking water for 19 million people for a year. So this kind of analysis can tell you that 10 gallons of trichloroethylene reaching an underground aquifer is not a small problem.

It's useful to know that a human's daily fluid intake averages two quarts, and the average human breathes 23 cubic meters of air daily.

If state and federal standards exist but are in conflict, give both. The public debate will be heated up, all to the good.

What if no standards exist, the case 9 times out of 10? You can only ask a series of fundamental questions of experts (or reference books) and try to put together a best guess.

Is this material toxic? How does it get into the environment? Is it vented into the air, discharged into sewage systems, disposed of as wastes?

Is it soluble in water? If so it tends to be mobile—the world is a wet place. *What water supplies could this contamination reach? What towns take their water from this water supply? What's the effect on drinking water?*

Is it soluble in lipids—fatty tissue—like DDT? This makes our bodies repositories.

Will it enter food chains and concentrate? We're at the top of many chains.

Is it likely to become airborne as a gas or dust? Will it then go into the lungs and pass into the bloodstream?

Will it break down — biodegrade — in the environment, or stay around a long time? How long? Are any of its breakdown products also toxic?

If you can learn or determine a *lethal dose (LD)* or *toxic dose,* divide it into the total amount of the substance involved to determine the total number of doses you're dealing with. Example: One ounce of plutonium 239 is enough to contaminate nearly 47 million people to the maximum permissible level. (Plans for nuclear waste dumps call for putting several million pounds underground.)

What are this substance's hazards to the environment other than human health impact? Can it migrate into groundwater? Can it kill fish, birds, insects, or plants — other than its target species, if a pesticide? *What studies have been conducted to gauge these things?*

When officials say there is no immediate threat to public health, ask: *Is there any delayed hazard that may become apparent in the future?* There often is. When officials say they have no evidence of hazard, ask: *Has anyone looked?* That is, has anyone made actual studies, including experiments in animals or bacteria or, one hopes, long-range studies in humans?

Beware of *safe averages* (most often heard about radioactive materials). We encounter hazards as individuals or small groups. Defenders of a low-level radioactive waste incinerator said it emitted tritium (radioactive hydrogen) but only a negligible fraction of 1 percent of the naturally occurring tritium in the atmosphere. The proper comparison would have been between natural background levels of tritium in ordinary air and tritium in the air downwind of the incinerator. That's where local people would breathe it.

Ask: *Who bears the risk and who gets the benefit?* Risk-benefit and cost-benefit analyses often add up total benefits but ignore these questions: Who benefits? Who pays? Who's at risk? And ask: *Have those who will bear the risk given their informed consent?*

The next time some official tells the public some hazard is negligible or nonhazardous, ask: *Would you raise your children in its presence?* Would you let them breathe it daily or drink it or spread it in your garden and feed them the vegetables?

Dr. Montague's last suggestion raises the hackles of some scientists who get asked, "What would you do?" or "What should we do?" They complain, "Too many investigators extrapolate beyond the results of their study. Our job is to bring out the facts, not speculate or extrapolate to decision making."

Most scientists, I believe, would disagree. It is true that some scientists trade on their reputations to pose as authorities on every question. Yet when someone who has studied the subject and conducted the experiments says, "Substance A causes cancer in laboratory animals," who can better give us some informed opinion on the best personal and public policy for the moment?

Reporters must ask: *Would you eat or drink substance A?* Or: *What are you doing about it? What do you think the public should do?* After all, the scientist is free to answer or not or reply, "I don't know enough yet to say."

To those who say, "We don't know the answers," you might ask: *Are you going to try to find out? Are you — or is someone — going to start a study of health effects? Who will do it, and are they experienced at such studies?*

When there is an accident or environmental or chemical problem: *Who is legally responsible for compensation, for a cleanup, for a solution? What is going to be done immediately or as soon as possible to decontaminate or try to control this problem? How is exposure —* in the workplace, in the general environment — *to be controlled in the future?*

When someone says, "This solution will be state-of-the-art, the very best technology can do," it may be true. But the right question in this case is, *Is this an adequate solution —* for public health and safety and for protection of the environment? For example, even the most modern landfills will ultimately leak; landfilling is not an adequate solution to chemical waste disposal.

Also ask: *Is the solution workable?* Have the management and operation been well thought out? Has human error been anticipated? Will there be continuous monitoring for some unexpected release?

And: *What will happen when someone, inevitably, makes a serious error?* To quote columnist Ellen Goodman, "We are stuck here in the high-tech, high-risk world with our own low-tech species."

Advice from Reporters

Here is some practical advice on these methods from reporters and others.

What we need to tell people, basically, are the answers to these questions:

- Is it a risk?
- If so, how great or small?
- Under what circumstances?
- How certain is this?
- What are the alternatives?

"Public health," says an editorial in the *American Journal of Public Health*, "has never clung to the principle that complete knowledge about a potential health hazard is a prerequisite for action."[13] When public health is threatened, seek the best available interpretation and advice available now.

When controversy rages, talk to people on all sides, of course. When possible, try to get scientists with opposing views to ask each other questions face-to-face.

But also try to find the best-informed, best-regarded scientists on the issue, including those who have themselves done actual testing or study, and some outside the controversy. Report: What is their advice? What is the *consensus?* Which way is the wind blowing?

Include the uncertainties that virtually always exist in any analysis or solution. If all the studies are weak, say so. If no one knows, say so.

Report probabilities — or the *range* of possibilities or probabilities — rather than just that mainstay of jazzy leads, the worst case. This is also called the "as many as" lead (example: "As many as a jillion could be killed"). This is not to say that worst cases should not be included—or sometimes be the lead of the story—if there is a good enough reason, not just a grab for a headline. But as William Ruckelshaus puts it, insist that risk estimates be presented as distributions of estimates to show the range of probabilities and not as magic numbers where no magic exists.

Put numbers on risks if at all possible, rather than just saying the risk is small or greater or greater than. Is the risk 1 in 100 or 1,000 or 1,000,000 or what? And per what unit of time? A day, a month, a year, or a lifetime?

Personalize the numbers. In addition to saying "the U.S. homicide death rate is 10.4 per 100,000 per year," you can say "the risk is 1 in 10,000" or "one person in every 10,000 will be a homicide victim."

Don't forget the denominators. If your headline reads, "20 Stricken in Epidemic," report 20 out of how many. What was the rate? And the total number at risk?

Ask: Is it the right denominator or comparison? Robert Hooke writes, "In a country of 200 million people, any very rare event can be made to sound commonplace by . . . telling how many people it happens to." His example of what he calls this broad-base fallacy: "the impression that travel on U.S. highways has become steadily more dangerous," though actually there has been a "continuously decreasing death rate per vehicle or per passenger mile."[14]

That's one way to look at it, of course. But one also finds that while the chance of being killed in any single auto trip is only about 1 in 4 million, we make some 50,000 trips in a lifetime, meaning that if we live, on the average, to age 75, we have 1 chance in 66 of dying in an auto accident.[15]

In 1985 there were four major crashes on U.S. scheduled airlines with 197 passenger deaths. A poor year without question. But the actual death roll per flight or departure—174 passenger deaths in 5.7 million flights—was about 1 death per 32,750 flights. More meaningful for anyone aboard a plane for takeoff, the actual risk was 1 chance in 1.4 million (5,700,000 ÷ 4 = 1,425,000) that that plane would crash on that flight. (Assessments of airline safety are often made in deaths per passenger miles, but many analysts consider deaths per departure a more meaningful figure, because most accidents occur on takeoff or landing.) The risk, of course, is multiplied by the number of takeoffs if you're on a flight with more than one takeoff and landing. It is multiplied by 50 if you're a frequent flyer who makes 50 such flights a year, making your risk 1 chance in 28,500. Not trivial. Still, says one epidemiologist, "people commonly overestimate the risks of air travel."

Compare risks when appropriate. Examples, considering in each case all Americans at risk per year and using approximate figures (rates change from year to year): the average risk of dying as a motor vehicle passenger is 1 in 5,000; of being fatally hit while crossing the street, 1 in 26,000; of being killed by a tornado, 1 in 450,000; of being killed by lightning, 1 in 1,000,000; of being killed by a bee sting, 1 in 5,500,000. I say, "All Americans at risk"—theoretically, anyone could be stung by a bee, even in Times Square—but if you're a farmer or beekeeper or gardener, your chances go up. The average isn't average for everybody.

Let Douglas Hofstadter round out this discussion: "Can you imagine how we would react if someone said . . . 'Hey, everybody! I've come up with a really nifty invention. Unfortunately it has a minor defect—every 13 years or so it will wipe out about as many Americans as the population of San Francisco!' That's what automobile accidents do."[16] Distinguish, however, between risks that we choose to accept and those imposed on us.

When we sometimes must accept some risks—for example, when the Food and Drug Administration declares a prescription drug "safe"—perhaps we should qualify the oversimple and misleading word "safe" and more accurately say "largely safe" or "relatively safe." Or try to indicate the degree of safety—or risk. We can also add the rates of adverse events.

Reporting scientific and technological risks requires *scientific and technological fact.* Read. Learn. Cultivate long-term sources—physicists, chemists, biologists, engineers, informed officials—who will be far easier to tap, and far more forthcoming, once they know you've done some homework.

Double-check facts. We journalists don't much like advice on doing our job, but Montague, once a journalist, says, "A recurring and bitterly felt complaint among scientists is that journalists often misquote, take words out of context, and fail to report qualifying phrases. Scientists can have their reputations tarnished by wrong-sounding statements attributed to them. Use a tape recorder to get their nuances—scientific language assigns words strict meanings. Then read back relevant passages." But make it clear first that you'll remain in control.

Don't forget people. Jim Detjen of the *Philadelphia Inquirer* says, "Write about things in a way your readers can relate to. Don't say rain has a pH [a measure of acidity or alkalinity] of 3; say it has become as acidic as vinegar. Don't just say so many parts per million of sulfur dioxide are going into the air; explain how these levels can trigger asthmatic attacks among sick and elderly.

"Find and write about environmental victims. But don't be irresponsible. You don't need to sensationalize. An accurate portrait is often alarming enough."[17]

Follow up and follow up and follow up," Detjen adds. Environmental problems don't go away. Is substance X still a problem? What, if anything, has been done a few years down the road?

I would add that the one-shot exposé, without sustained follow-up, is a common media sin. It does little good to expose a problem about the environment or anything else unless you stay with it. Follow the nitty-gritty of administrative, legislative, industry, or community action and report what, if anything, gets done.

Use your own judgment. Dr. Dorothy Nelkin at Cornell University says, "The most serious problem" in reporting on risk "may be less one of bias, inaccuracy and sensationalism" than the reluctance of technically vulnerable journalists to challenge their sources and "those who use the authority of science to shape the public view." Maintain "the spirit of independent, critical inquiry that has guided good investigation in other areas."[18]

The Statistics of Politics, Economics, and Democracy

9

Sound policies rest on good information.

—Dr. Frederick Mosteller

Statistics are the heart of democracy.

—Simeon Strunsky

"Go on, Mrs. Pratt," says Mrs. Sampson. "Them ideas is so original and soothing. I think statistics are just as lovely as they can be."

—O. Henry

THE word "statistics" comes from the Latin meaning "to stand"—or "status" or "state of things." Statistics tell us how things stand. A scholar of mathematics says, "The German word *Statistik,* from which the subject derives its name, was used by its coiner in 1749" to mean a "science of state." The word "state" comes from the same Latin root, and H. G. Wells once said that "statistical thinking"—the ability to tell how things stand, including the ability to manage a state—"will one day be as necessary for efficient citizenship as the ability to read and write."

At the least, we have seen, we can rather easily learn quite a bit about telling an honest statistic from a canard and an honest number cruncher from a snake-oil salesman, statesmen included. The same rules for recognizing reasonably credible

126

statements in science, medicine, and the environment apply to recognizing them in government, politics, and economics. Or in advertising or any other area. The same kind of questions apply: How do you know? Have you done a study? What kind? What numbers lead you to your conclusions? How valid, how reliable, how probable are they? Compared with what?

Florence Nightingale knew this. Far more than a Lady With a Lamp, she applied statistics as well as tenderness to running a hospital. A biographer called her "a Passionate Statistician." In 1891, bemoaning government's failure to collect and use statistics as a guide to policy, she wrote Sir Francis Galton: "You remember what [Adolphe] Quetelet [mid-19th-century Belgian scientist and mathematician who has been called the leading precursor of the modern statistician] wrote. . . . 'Put down what you expect from such and such legislation; after − − years, see where it has given you what you expected, and where it has failed. But you change your laws and your administering of them so fast, and without an inquiry after results past or present, that it is all experiment, see-saw, doctrinaire, a shuttlecock between two battledores.' "[1]

Were she alive and transported to America, Miss Nightingale might be happier today but once again disturbed. The U.S. government has the world's largest, most far-ranging statistical apparatus. It is in many ways magnificent yet often wanting in light of current needs. During the late 1970s and 1980s it suffered in an era preoccupied with trimming back, and also demeaning, "bureaucracy" in all areas but defense. The cutbacks included statistics gathering. Never mind that you can't get more bang for the buck in any area unless you know how big the bang.

More on this later. Meanwhile, government officials — federal and local — are constantly telling us, "We have learned that . . . ," "Statistics show . . . ," and, now, "The computer showed. . . ." Words and computers show nothing. They depend on numbers, which depend not only on quantity and timeliness but also on the right way of collecting them, comparing them, and analyzing them and the right assumptions about the world they describe. There is every reason to apply some of our good-sense tests to such statements and to some common attempts, by government officials and others, to pull statistics over our eyes.

We are often hindered, those many of us who have not had much math or were poor at math, by a fear of numbers. It may help us to couch some statistical principles in more common language, such as "what's missing?" In 1954 Darrell Huff wrote a small book called *How to Lie With Statistics.* [2] Huff boils down some statistical and other sound thinking in a chapter called "How to Talk Back to a Statistic" — that is, "how to look a phony statistic in the eye and face it down and, no less important, how to recognize sound and usable data."

He recommends asking the following "five simple questions" and insisting on answers:

(1) *"Who says so?"* Look for the biased source, he says, "the laboratory with something to prove for the sake of a theory, a reputation or a fee; the newspaper whose aim is a good story; labor or management with a wage level at stake." Bias may be conscious — outright misstatement, ambiguous statement, selection of favorable or unfavorable data, or use of an improper measure such as a mean (the arithmetical average) where a median would be more informative. Or the bias may be unconscious, "often more dangerous."

It may "take at least a second look to find out who says so," Huff says, for "the who may be hidden" by what author Stephen Potter called an "O.K. name" — "anything smacking of the medical profession," a scientific laboratory, a college or university. In short, just because Dr. X of Harvard says it doesn't make it so. (See *bias, mean/median/mode,* Chapter 3.)

(2) *"How does he know?"* Watch for statements based on inadequate or biased samples. There may not be enough cases "to convince any reasoning person of anything." There may be a sample that "has selected itself." During the Korean War a busi-

ness newspaper reported that of 169 corporations that had replied to a poll on "price gouging," two thirds said they were absorbing wartime price increases. It turned out that only 14 percent of the firms had replied; 86 percent had not answered. (See " 'Power' and Numbers" Chapter 3; *sampling,* Chapter 4.)

(3) *"What's missing?"* "You won't always be told how many cases" or be given a measure of reliability (a probability value or confidence limits) or some other figure needed for comparison. A major corporation reported an annual profit after taxes of "only" 12.6 percent. The company's unstated profit on investment was 44.8 percent. Huff quotes a critic of this kind of legerdemain: "If I purchase an article every morning for 99 cents and sell it each afternoon for $1, I will make only 1 percent on total sales, but 365 percent on invested money during the year."

"What's missing" frequently is an alternative explanation—in statistical language, an unstated or unknown confounding variable. A business story says that April retail sales were well ahead of April's the year before. Left unstated: the fact that Easter came in March the first year and in April the second. (See *probability values, confounding variables,* Chapter 3.)

(4) *"Did somebody change the subject?"* Watch for a switch somewhere between a raw figure and the conclusion. "One thing is all too often reported as another. . . . More reported cases of a disease are not always the same thing as more cases. . . . An expressed preference by a 'cross-section' of a magazine's readers for articles on world affairs is not final proof that they would read them." The 1950 census found more 65-to-70-year-olds than there were 55-to-60-year-olds 10 years earlier. Immigration could not explain the difference. Authorities believed there was probably much falsifying of ages by people eager to collect the Social Security payments that began in 1940, or much truth telling by Social Security eligibles whose earlier age reports were products of vanity.

(5) *"Does it make sense?"* This test will often "cut a statistic down to size," Huff tells us. Some years ago a well-known urolo-

gist said there were 8 million cases of prostate cancer in the United States. A reporter calculated that that would have meant one case for every male in the susceptible age group.

Another good rule, per Huff: "A difference is a difference only if it makes a difference."

Statistician Nancy Lyon Spruill, writing in the *Washington Post,* described many of these statistical lessons as various politicians' tricks (although these statistical shenanigans are by no means confined to politicians):[3]

(1) *The everything's-going-up statistic.* More people are employed, or more people are getting support payments or whatever. Right, because there are more people than ever. A more informative statistic is the employment or unemployment *rate* or the portion of the population getting welfare payments.

A variant: saying the median family income rose from one year to the next by $X or X percent. Adjust for inflation to get constant dollars, and you may find that real income dropped.

An Agriculture Department official hailed the finding that pork exports had tripled in a two-month period. Another official cautioned that the apparent sharp increase could be misleading—as it eventually proved to be—because few pork products were exported and anytime "you start off with a small base, the percentage increase is going to be large."[4]

(2) *The best-foot statistic.* Selecting whatever number best supports a case, as in choosing between median and mean family income. If the rich get richer and the poor get poorer, the median might stay unchanged. If a few get richer, the mean income will be dragged up, even if incomes for most families remain unchanged.

Also: picking the best-sounding year for comparison. To show an increase in family income, for example, you can compare the prosperous present with a deep recession year.

The Secretary of the Navy said in late 1985 that the cost of Navy aircraft had been on the decline thanks to "vigorous cost management," and he sent charts to Congress to prove it. A whistle-blowing Pentagon cost analyst pointed out that the charts covered only the period from fiscal 1982 to fiscal 1985, which ended in midyear, and stopped just before costs jumped up. And not only that. The major aircraft supplier had appeared to be charging less by shifting part of the bill from production to research, for which the taxpayers also paid. The whistle-blower conceded that there was "a small kernel of truth," but it was swamped by "embellished simplifications."[5]

(3) *The gee-whiz or half-truth statistic.* Example: using numbers for only part of the population. If the unemployment rate doesn't say what you want, talk about the rate for teenagers or the rate in industrialized states. Or to deplore defense spending, tell how increases in defense spending have increased the national debt, but don't mention nondefense increases or the effect of changes up or down in taxation.

(4) *The anecdote statistic.* How Mrs. Gladpenny benefited from some juggling that left a larger proportion of the population below the poverty level.

(5) *The everyone-is-average statistic.* We're told that women can't be combat soldiers or fire fighters because the average man can lift more weight than the average woman. But many a woman can and does lift more weight than many a man.

(6) *The coincidence statistic.* How two things have increased or decreased over time, so one must have led to the other. Whoever is in office is blamed for a recession, though economists can't agree on the cause. Whoever is in office takes credit for a boom, though ditto.

Fortune writer Daniel Seligman, in an article titled "We're Drowning in Phony Statistics," warned of two variants:[6]

• *The meaningless statistic,* as when the mayor of New York City says that "overall cleanliness of the streets has risen to 85 per cent," up from 56 percent in five years. By what objective criteria? Neither the mayor nor his aides could come up with any, though suitable measurements could have been devised.

• *The unknowable statistic,* which is discoverable—like the above—by simply asking, "How do you know?"

Politicians, we see, love to use the most beguiling statistic: a total increase or decrease if it sounds better than the rate of change, the rate of change if it sounds better than the numbers, a misleading base or no base (no "compared with what"). The antidote to all these offenses: Ask for *all* the numbers, then see if they are appropriate ones for drawing any conclusions. Calculate your own rates of change from what seem to be sensible bases. Look at changes over several, not just a few, years. Keep asking, How do you know?

"If you're going to use a number," advises *Newsweek's* economics columnist, Robert Samuelson, "you'd better know where it comes from, how reliable it is and whether it means what it seems to mean. The garbage-in, garbage-out problem has been with us a long time. Or as British economist Sir Josiah Stamp (1880–1941) once put it: 'The Government [is] very keen on amassing statistics. They collect them, add them, raise them to the nth power, take the cube root and prepare wonderful diagrams. But you must never forget that every one of these figures comes in the first instance from the village watchman, who just puts down what he damn well pleases.'"[7]

Data-gathering is far better today, but there are still garbagemen.

Again and again some overall statistic is loudly trumpeted, but some of the most revealing numbers are buried in the tables and often not mentioned in briefings or press releases. Remember to *stratify* or *disaggregate*—to dig beneath the averages—to examine important parts of a large population. (See *stratification,* Chapter 4.)

In Chapter 4, we said that merely reporting that elderly Americans are "no longer [an economically] disadvantaged group" conceals that they are also more likely to have below-average incomes. A spate of 1985 news stories that looked mainly at the elderly as a whole led to a widespread but mistaken impression that most of them were living on easy street. Although the poverty rate for the aged had dropped from 35.2

percent in 1959 to 12.1 percent in 1985, and the 1985 rate for the nation was 14 percent, later studies showed the following:[8]

• The elderly's poverty rate was higher than that of any other adult group and seemed lower than the national rate because the overall rate was swollen by a 20 percent rate among children.

• Two out of 10 elderly women who lived alone lived in poverty. So did 3 out of 10 elderly blacks, men and women.

• Many of the elderly, though not below the grim poverty line, were still economically vulnerable. Forty-two percent had incomes either at or below two times the poverty line; just 32.8 percent of the rest of society had similar income levels.

• Other studies have made it clear that "over 65" has itself become too broad a category for informed policy making. Those in their sixties and seventies may be doing fairly well on the whole, but there is a fast-growing group of the "older old" in their eighties and nineties who have run out of money and health.

In September 1985 the Census Bureau reported that the number of Americans of all ages living below the poverty line in 1984 had made a one-year drop from 15.3 to 14.4 percent, the first significant drop since 1976. True enough, meaning there were 1.8 million fewer poor people. President Reagan hailed this "as further proof that . . . America after a difficult decade is once again headed in the right direction."

But the following was not mentioned:

• The 1984 rate was still higher than that when Reagan took office in 1981, and it was higher than that in any year between 1970 and 1980. In the words of one analyst, "we may be at a new [high] plateau of poverty."

• While the 1984 median national income rose, the bottom 40 percent of families claimed only 15.7 percent of the total national income, and the top 40 percent got 67.3 percent, the highest portion ever recorded.

• The children's poverty rate, though down a bit from 1983, was still a third higher than in 1976 and 1977. Those particular numbers will be obsolete by the time you read this. But the problem they illustrate will be the same. The problem, says Commissioner of Labor Statistics Janet Norwood, is that "we tend to look for aggregate solutions"—based on the aggregate numbers—"and pay too little attention to the need for particular solutions for particular problems."[9]

In a mid-1987 article, *New York Times* reporter Clyde H. Farnsworth documented a few ways politicians can use alternative measurements—useful and informative for various purposes—for political purposes.[10]

• The Commerce Department described the June 1987 trade deficit as $15.7 billion, a record widely reported. Two days later a second report put the deficit at $14.1 billion. "A little-known provision of the Trade Act of 1979 required that the larger number, which adds insurance and freight charges to the landed cost of imports, be published 48 hours before the smaller. . . . The later report, which many economists say more accurately measures the nation's trading position by comparing only the value of the imported goods themselves with the value of exported goods, was largely ignored. . . . The initiators of the change were protectionist-leaning legislators led by Russell B. Long, former Democratic senator from Louisiana, who wanted the trade numbers to look as grim as possible to promote protectionist legislation."

• The Census Bureau in 1985 began issuing two reports on household income: its traditional annual report on median family income and a new one including noncash benefits like food stamps, government housing, and health care—though health care, in particular, is hardly "income" by most definitions, since people don't choose to be sick or wind up with more cash in pocket. "The second report takes longer to prepare. But the Reagan Administration, eager to show that it has reduced poverty, favors [it]. And so that a report of cash income alone does not steal the headlines, the administration two years ago persuaded the Census Bureau to issue both reports on the same day. . . . [The first report covering 1984] showed that 14.4 percent of the population was below the poverty line, but the other said that this dropped to 9.7 percent when the noncash benefits were incorporated as income. . . . The administration . . . cited a 'historic drop in poverty—the largest and most broadly based drop in poverty in over a decade.'" This methodology continues.

• The unemployment index, "one of the politically most sensitive," also has two versions. "President Reagan, boasting about economic achievements of his leadership, recently noted that the unemployment rate had fallen below 6 percent for the first time since 1979. He could not have said this, however, had the Bureau of Labor Statistics not accepted a recommendation from the National Commission on Employment and Unemployment Statistics in 1983 to incorporate the armed forces in the national workforce. . . . Actually the bureau reports unemployment as a percentage of both the civilian labor force and the total labor force. The difference is one-tenth of a percentage point. Against only the civilian labor pool, unemployment in July still stood at 6 percent; against the total pool, it was 5.9. But it obviously packed more of a punch for the President to talk of joblessness falling below the 6 percent threshold."

The point is not to decry multiple numbers that describe various aspects of the same subject. Differing indices can give us different, equally valuable information. The abuse comes when selected ones are used to make political capital.

"Statistics are the economy's flashlights," says Robert Samuelson, "but sometimes they illuminate poorly," requiring the analysis of an expert reporter. In July 1986 Samuelson noticed that prices of goods, led by oil, had been falling, while, according to the economic statistics, prices for services were rising at a "breezy" 5 percent annual rate. "It turns out," he wrote, "that high service inflation is an economic mirage, a quirk of statistics, not what's happening." The reason:

> Statistical anomalies . . . Consider home ownership. It represents a seventh of the CPI [Consumer Price Index] and almost a third of the index's service component. . . . Plunging interest rates . . . have sharply cut monthly payments. . . . But the CPI hasn't shown any decline. . . . The CPI doesn't measure home ownership costs directly, but assumes they change in parallel with rents on similar housing units. . . . Rents have . . . given a misleading picture of home owner costs. . . .
>
> There are other flaws. . . . Air fares are overstated because the CPI has failed to capture the shift to discount fares under deregulation. According to the CPI, air fares have risen two-thirds since 1980. But, in fact, the average fare today is near 1980 levels. . . .
>
> These technical problems can have large statistical effects. . . . The false picture of a stubborn services inflation has caused the Federal Reserve to hold interest rates too high for too long, . . . exaggerated inflation's staying power and . . . meant that excessive "real" interest rates—adjusted for actual, not statistical inflation—have hurt farmers and deterred business investment.[11]

Samuelson concluded that "the point is not to condemn" these statistics—the technical problems in gathering them are immense and "there's a danger in making quick changes"—"but to grasp their limits."

About those "real" interest rates. The interest rates we generally see—the naked, published figures—are the *nominal rates,* those we *think* we pay. The *real interest rate,* to an economist, is the difference between the nominal rate and the current inflation rate.

When the published interest rate was 18 percent, for example, inflation was running 12 percent but repayment was made in *lower real dollars*—dollars worth less because of inflation. So the real interest rate, the cost to those who must pay off loans, became just 6 percent. With a 12 percent interest rate and 4 percent inflation rate, the real interest rate becomes 8 percent, 2 points higher than in the time of greater inflation. A financial adviser says that if you earned 18 percent on your old certificate of deposit in a 14 percent inflation world, your real return was 4 percent, exactly the same as a 7 percent return with 3 percent inflation, this though "$1,800 on a $10,000 CD sure looked like a lot more than $700 on the same $10,000."

This analysis, of course, ignores another important element in determining the real cost of borrowing or the real benefit of an investment: the tax saving you may be able to get on interest payments or the tax you may have to pay on investment earnings, depending on your financial circumstances. When an administration says it has lowered interest rates, consider the real rates that people are paying—and how current tax laws might benefit or penalize various taxpayers.

Statistically minded thinking can throw light on the foreign news and the war news. Yale professor I. Richard Savage reminds us that the Foreign Assistance Act requires the State Department to report annually to Congress on the status of human rights in United Nations members and nations that we assist.[12] One measure used—refer to the news in the 1980s from El Salvador—is the number of political killings. Changes in the number of killings may not necessarily mean changes in policy, Savage warns. Reductions could also reflect the elimination of potential victims by the kind of disruption and emigration a torn country experiences (those who might be killed flee or go underground) as well as by attrition (there aren't as many targets left to be killed). Remember confounding variables.

Savage also remembers that the news of Vietnam "gave ample suggestion that statistics was being used for self-deception." He quotes then Defense Secretary Robert McNamara: "You couldn't reconcile the number of the enemy, the level of infiltration, the body count, and the resultant figures. It just didn't add up. I never did get . . . a balanced equation." Nor did perceptive reporters.

We breathlessly await and often are influenced by results of polls, political and otherwise, that attempt to tell us what we are thinking. At best, however, even with their sometimes stated (though often omitted) 95 percent certainty or 95 percent confidence level, there will be (1) 5 chances in 100 that an unrepresentative sample rather than truth determined the result and (2) a result that usually varies plus or minus 2 to 4 percentage points from the truth, depending on how large the sample (usually around 500 to 1,500). This means a 4-to-8-point area in which the real truth may repose *if* the pollster's sample is representative *and* the questions used have elicited something close to a valid and reliable response.

The questions asked in polls are crucial. They can be loaded to get a desired result. Or they can be innocently yet badly worded — hence enters bias — to get misleading answers. Pollsters' results vary widely even when they make their best, most expensive, most testable efforts to predict the results of elections. This happens in large part because the pollsters commonly *adjust* — change — their results according to the varying judgments and assumptions they make about possible voters and who will really turn out to vote. They also use different techniques, different ways of picking samples, and differently worded questions, all of which can mean differing results. Here, in a remarkable and commendable display of candor that you won't commonly see is how the *New York Times* qualified a New York City poll conducted in January 1987 with 900 adults:

> In theory, in 19 cases out of 20, the results based on such samples will differ by no more than 3 percentage points in either direction from that which would have been obtained by interviewing all adult New Yorkers. For smaller groups, the potential error is greater. For all whites, plus or minus 4 percentage points. For all blacks, it is plus or minus 7 points.
>
> In addition to sampling error, the practical difficulties of conducting any survey of public opinion may introduce other sources of error into the poll.[13]

Shouldn't everyone reporting polling results be as candid, at least once in a while? Within a few weeks in July 1984, five major polls gave President Reagan a lead varying from 1 to 26 points over Walter Mondale. Who was near the mark at that point? We have no idea. But in their final, most careful predictions on election eve, seven polls gave the president leads that varied from 10 to 25 points. He won by 18 points. The veteran Louis Harris, off 6 points, said he had chosen to rely on his last day of polling instead of the last three days, which had generally proved more accurate in the past.[14] At best, says pollster Richard Wirthlin, polling is an " 'ABC' science, almost being certain," because "we are not dealing with reality directly, but through a mirror darkly clouded."[15]

Poll results may also be variously quoted by persons bent on showing one thing or another. Again, to quote Samuelson: "To prove the popularity of President Reagan's tax plan, you cite surveys showing that roughly half of the public favor it, with about a third against. To demonstrate opposition, you cite polls indicating large majorities against specific proposals, such as the elimination of the deduction for local taxes. In fact, inconsistent results often indicate just that: the public is ambivalent."[16]

The subject of sex shows that there are pollsters and pollsters. In 1987 author and social investigator Shere Hite published her third book on men and women in bed and out. Hite's latest findings — on women's attitudes about men, sex, and personal and marital relationships — put her on the cover of *Time* and launched a flood of news stories and TV talk.

Hite had distributed 100,000 detailed questionnaires, seeking answers to 127 questions, to women in groups of many kinds all over the country. She received only 4,500 replies. On the basis of those, she reported that 84 percent of the women in her study were dissatisfied with their marital or other intimate relationships, that 78 percent said they were generally not treated as equals by men, and that 70 percent of those married more than five years had had affairs. And so on, with a number of answers and Hite's elaborations indicating that women in general are mainly unhappy with their relationships.

Women in general? Hite said at one point in her book that "no one can generalize" from her findings. Yet she also claimed that her 4,500 respondents were typical of all American women, and she said her results "could be replicated" on a far larger scale with no more than a 10 percent difference in results. Critics — virtually all social scientists and students of public opinion who commented — said her sample was almost certainly heavily weighted with the unhappiest women, those who took the time to answer the lengthy questionnaire. The critics did not doubt that many women feel the same way as Hite's respondents. They just did not know how many.

Testing Hite's findings, a *Washington Post*–ABC News polling team questioned a representative sample — representative by usual polling methods — of 767 women and 738 men across the nation. That poll found that 93 percent of the married and single women said they were satisfied with their relationships, 81 percent said they were treated as equals most of the time, and only 7 percent reported affairs. That survey, like most surveys, was conducted by phone. Hite said women would not be candid to a telephone caller. Jeff Alderman, ABC polling director, replied, "Over the phone, people will say things to us they wouldn't say to a neighbor. We've never had any indication they lie." But Richard Morin, *Washington Post* polling director, conceded that these sunny results should be interpreted with some care too, since "telephone surveys like this might be expected to overstate satisfaction with personal relationships, and understate, to a significantly greater degree, the extent of socially unacceptable behavior such as adultery."[17]

Who was closer to the truth? I don't know, but we do know that telephone surveys of small, well-selected samples can at least come within hail of the truth when they are severely tested in elections. Hite, in contrast, is no scientific sampler of public opinion. She nonetheless uncovered hundreds of revealing stories and strong emotions. We deserve a look as deep and searching as hers at male-female relationships, but — so important is the subject — one with results as valid as the most careful political poll.

Reporters love predictions. Be cautious. "The species *homo sapiens* has a powerful propensity to believe that one can find a pattern even when there is no pattern to be found" — when random variability or chance produces what only seems to be a pattern. So writes Dr. Julian L. Simon, University of Maryland economist.[18]

Take baseball, he says. A generally good hitter strikes out three or four consecutive times at bat. The coach then declares a "slump" and pulls him out of the lineup. But studies show that short-term performance in most sports varies in the same way that a run of random numbers or coin flips varies. Similarly, it has been shown, a basketball player's chance of making a basket on each try is unaffected by whether he made or missed the previous shot.

Take the stock market, says Simon, where "hundreds of thousands of investors pay high prices for market letters that purport to be systems for finding patterns. . . . Others purchase the analyses of 'chartists' who see in stock prices . . . patterns that they claim tell you when to buy and sell. . . . According to [a] massive body of statistical analyses . . . rules based on such chartist patterns have zero validity." But a few persons pick a portfolio of stocks that almost universally go up, just as a few people among many coin-flippers will flip several heads in a row.

Take government policy, where "many government officials misunderstand chance variability at great cost to the public." Simon's example: "The farmers of the country suffered terribly for their mistaken faith in forecasts that land and food prices would continue going up, based on short-run observations during the 1970s."

There are indeed long-range trends in sports and the economy. A good player becomes a poor or aging one. Land prices grow over the long run as population grows and land becomes scarcer. But beware of short-term predictions or hasty diagnoses of batters' slumps or economic trends. As one statistician puts it: "Even though there may be real trends in a system, many systems inherently have a very large random component which over short terms may obscure the long-term trends."[19] (See "Variability," Chapter 3.)

Robert Hooke warns us about ads, not very different from many political claims, that say, "Independent laboratory tests show that no other leading product is more effective than ours." His translation: "A [purposely] small test was run among the leading products, and no significant difference was observed among the products tested. . . . There are people around who can make good news for themselves out of anything."[20]

Darrell Huff tells of a juice extractor widely advertised as one that "extracts 26 percent more juice." More than what? Inquiry showed "only that this juicer got that much more juice than an old-fashioned hand reamer," though it still might be the poorest electric juicer on the market.

Another example from Huff: "Users report 23 percent fewer cavities with Doakes' toothpaste. . . . The principal joker in this one is the inadequate sample. . . . That test group of users consisted of just a dozen persons." Another way Doakes may fool the public is by quietly financing test after test in small groups where "sooner or later, by the operation of chance, a test group is going to show a big improvement."

Or, per Huff: "If you can't prove what you want to prove, demonstrate something else and pretend that they are the same thing. . . . You can't prove that your nostrum cures colds, but you can publish a sworn laboratory report that half an ounce of the stuff killed 31,108 germs in a test tube. . . . It is not up to you — is it? — to point out that an antiseptic that works well in a test tube may not perform in the human throat. . . . [And] don't confuse the issue by telling what kind of germ you killed."

Or if the stuff really affected colds, not just some germs, in a well-conducted, well-controlled study.[21]

Lessons: Small studies cannot reach strong conclusions. Single, unreplicated studies can seldom prove anything. Chance—random variation—can do strange things to study results. The results of poor studies can be dressed up in misleading language. (See Chapter 4.)

Do a little arithmetic. On July 19, 1986, the *New York Times* reported on page one, "White Americans, whose incomes are almost twice those of blacks, have accumulated 10 times as much wealth, according to a study the Census Bureau published today." UPI reported "more than 10 times as much wealth"; *Newsweek,* "almost 12 times"; the *Washington Post,* "12."[22] None was quite correct. The precise figure was 11.52 times as great (a median net household worth for whites of $39,135; for blacks, $3,397). I'd have rounded it to 11.5.

Watch your reporting. An experienced editor says,

A lot of reporters don't realize what random selection means. For instance, they'll set out to collect opinion on a political candidate or seek opinions on any subject. They'll make this common mistake. They'll ask somebody—somebody picked at random, perhaps—a question, but then take *that* person's recommendation on the next person to talk to, because the first person has said, "I'll tell you somebody else who knows a lot about that."

At that point they no longer have a random sample. I think the expression for this is a snowball sample. What made me aware of it was a survey we had a couple of professors do, a survey of Vietnamese refugees in this country about their treatment in refugee camps back in Vietnam. They interviewed one family, then that family knew another family, and so on. They soon realized they were getting only one story and changed their methodology. It makes you realize how easily you can skew things.[23]

A statistician adds: True enough and worth guarding against. But snowball sampling can be a good way to collect information about a particular class of persons with the same interests or problems. Just don't confuse them with a representative sample of a broader population.

Don't bury the numbers if the numbers are the story.

A page-one story in the *New York Times* told me that "workers at New York City building sites have the highest rate of death from unsafe conditions among the nation's 35 largest cities."[24] How many workers have been dying? I had to read to the 14th paragraph, on the jump page inside the second section, to learn that from 1979 through 1985 the numbers of deaths varied from 7 to 15 a year. I had to get to the 25th paragraph to find the *rate* described in the first paragraph: 7.61 deaths for each billion dollars of construction, much higher than the average 3.3 deaths in the 35 cities. Why couldn't the lead have told me right at the outset, "Between 7 and 15 New York City workers a year die in construction accidents"? Fear of numbers? Fear that even *New York Times* readers fear numbers? Fear that 7 to 15 deaths a year wouldn't sound impressive in the big, violent city? I don't know.

Why is the reporting of true numbers and the whole truth about them so important? Underreporting or misinterpretation can lead to misunderstanding and bad personal, social, and political decisions.

The reporting of AIDS is an important example. Health officials were widely quoted in 1987 as saying that the chance that the AIDS virus will spread in a single act of heterosexual intercourse is extremely low, perhaps 1 in 1,000. Accurate enough, as far as it went. But as Professor Joseph Gastwirth of George Washington University pointed out, to convert that single exposure risk of 1 in 1,000 to real, long-range risk, one needs to consider the possible frequency of intercourse.[25] Assuming that the probability of transmission is the same in every contact, the risk after 100 contacts would be roughly 10 percent, or 1 chance in 10—a much more impressive and dangerous risk than one chance in 1,000.

Almost no medical test is without false positives and false negatives, such are biological variation and observer and instrument error. There has been little mention of that in scores of news stories about the possibility, and possible wisdom, of widespread or compulsory AIDS testing. Of every 100,000 1987 tests of military applicants, about 150 were positive. But between 1 and 3 of each 150 (or between 0.67 and 2 percent) were false positives, as determined by elaborate rechecks. The life of each individual so falsely labeled might be drastically and erroneously changed because of the false diagnosis. There were fewer false negatives, only a fraction of 1 percent at several competent laboratories, yet those too pose obvious dangers.

The above were the false-positive and false-negative rates, moreover, in some of the nation's best labs, with rigorous standards. In an article in the *New England Journal of Medicine,* Tufts Drs. Stephen Pauker and Klemens Meyer predicted in mid-1987 that false-positive rates would rise as lower-quality laboratories were used or if increased demand overburdened laboratories. They said that in groups with very low risk of infection—for example, couples about to be married—the false-positive rate might be so high that false positives outnumbered true positives.

The false-positive rate is certain to go up to some extent as testing is done in more laboratories with uneven methods, Pauker predicted in an interview, and "it doesn't have to go up very much to create a social catastrophe." In their article, Pauker and Meyer asked, "How many jobs should be lost? How many insurance policies should be canceled or denied? How many fetuses should be aborted and how many couples should remain childless to avert the birth of one child with AIDS?"[26]

Society must of course attempt to curtail the spread of so devastating a disease. The policy making will never become easy, but the reporting surely ought to include pertinent statistics like these and their ramifications.

The State of the Nation's Statistics

What are the chances that we reporters, better informed, will do better? Any reporter who covers governments in a town, city, county, or state or in Washington or Timbuktu knows that a frequent answer to a request for factual, including statistical, information is "We don't know." Will that increasingly be the answer we hear? In 1986 Congressional testimony and in report after report (including one by the bipartisan Joint Economics Committee of Congress) a series of statisticians, economists, and others said:

• The ability of the federal government—the prime collector of national and local statistics—to track what was happening throughout society and the economy was deteriorating.

• The downslide began in the Carter years and accelerated in the Reagan era with "assaults on useless bureaucrats," "a generally demeaning attitude toward federal employees," and "arbitrary and ill-considered budget cutting" in nearly all statistical agencies.

• As a result, agencies were collecting less information, cutting sample sizes, reducing the frequency and scope of statistics gathering, adding to already great delays in publishing results, and cutting back on distribution. Coordination of statistics gathering, once an important function of the White House Office of Management and Budget (OMB), had been almost destroyed.

• All in all, the government had been "cutting into meat and not fat," basing crucial policies on inaccurate or nonexistent data, and failing to keep pace with the nation's rapid social and economic changes.

Amazingly, in 1984 a key OMB official said, "Each of these information collections [throughout the government] requires the expenditure of public and private resources that might be more profitably spent. . . . The more money we spend to collect, process, and disseminate information, the less there is available for private services."

That position—by an administration also seeking to "privatize" and sell much information that most authorities believed could most effectively be gathered by the government—was officially revised. The attitude was not. According to Katherine Wallman, director of a concerned council of statistical, economic, health, industrial, and scholarly groups, the philosophy in the administration and the OMB had become one that "suggests that information collection activities are in the first instance a burden, something to be eliminated regardless of the usefulness of the data."

The following were among the consequences of that attitude and earlier deficiencies, according to these and other witnesses:

• Unreliable "reliability studies" of nuclear power plants, increasing the danger of nuclear accidents.

• Self-deception of the Navy. For lack of good statistical support, it believed that it had higher mission readiness rates for its aircraft than it really had.

• Lack of current data on hunger and the nutritional status of Americans.

• "Woefully inadequate" data on illegal immigrants, with 1985 federal estimates of their numbers ranging all the way from 3.5 million to 7 million. Part of the problem is getting these numbers without expensive, draconian methods. But a National Research Council panel called the Immigration and Naturalization Service's record keeping "Dickensian . . . indeed clumsier than that used by clerks of the Cratchit era."

• Lack of an information base by which "the state and performance of the American educational system," whether good, bad, indifferent, improving, or worsening, could be accurately assessed. Two examples: There had been no accurate estimate of illiterates. There had been no state-by-state comparisons of student knowledge and skills, so the residents of any state might know how their students compared with others.

• Lack of knowledge of Americans' current health. The nation was spending $500 billion a year on health care as of mid-1987, but only a tiny part of that was being spent on trying to learn the results or study the best ways of care. Dr. David Rogers, then president of the Robert Wood Johnson Foundation, said,

In health care, even fairly simple statistics are not regularly collected, or when they are, they are processed so slowly that they are not available until two to five years after the fact. Thus in most communities no one knows how often individuals are seen by their doctors or how many mothers are receiving pregnancy care or whether the changes we are making in . . . the delivery of care are resulting in more or fewer infant deaths or deaths from heart disease or cancer or diabetes or what-have-you.

Example: The National Center for Health Statistics had to start conducting its National Ambulatory Care Survey every five years instead of every three years, and its survey of nursing care, every nine years instead of three to five years.

"There is little doubt that serious under-reporting exists" in the government's estimates of occupationally related illness, a National Research Council panel concluded. To quote a summary of the panel's findings: "The accuracy of even the most basic information collected by the federal government on occupational injuries, including the number of fatal injuries, is unknown. No adequate studies have been conducted to check employer reports of injuries against independent sources of information, such as death certificates or hospital records. . . . The lack of validated statistics hampers the Department of Labor's Occupational Safety and Health Administration (OSHA) from maintaining an effective program for prevention of workplace injuries and illnesses." It is "rather startling," the panel said, "that an agreed-upon method has not been devised to estimate a phenomenon as basic as traumatic death in the workplace."[27]

Rates for many kinds of surgery vary widely—or wildly—

both from state to state and from county to county within states, the classic studies of Dr. John Wennberg of Dartmouth and others have shown. There were few adequate studies to try to learn why.

The federal government in 1985 began a revolutionary new system of paying hospitals only a fixed sum, regardless of length of stay, for virtually all Medicare patients. Other insurers moved in similar directions, and hospitals began sending elderly patients home earlier. Yet there existed no pre-1985 knowledge base — no adequate measurements of hospital outcomes or deaths — by which to learn whether these drastic new "cost-containment" programs were harming or helping patients. As of this writing, there were still only scattered efforts and, in the opinion of many observers, no comprehensive, well-funded program to establish even a current information base adequate to investigate the question, Are the new programs making patients better or sicker?

The fact that millions of Americans lack any or adequate health insurance is often called a national disgrace. Yet no one knew the true number of uninsured — there were perhaps 30 million, perhaps 37 million. Even more broadly, by one assessment, "we have no idea how much access or lack of access there is to medical care — a great impediment to planning."

• Lack of information about the economy. "Our basic economic framework, the economic statistics framework, is deteriorating" . . . "Federal agencies are not collecting as much data" . . . "The government's measurements frequently give a distorted picture."

The Leading Economic Indicators, watched closely with "an impact on millions of daily decisions," became "inconsistent . . . unreliable forecasters . . . often subject to wildly swinging revisions" — for lack of basic revision in more than a decade. The *Wall Street Journal* reported in December 1985, for example,

The Commerce Department released revised GNP [figures] showing that growth in the fourth quarter of 1984, which at the time appeared to be moving along briskly at a 4.3 per cent inflation adjusted annual rate, was actually crawling at an anemic six-tenths of 1 per cent rate, and GNP growth in the first quarter of 1985 turned out to be 3.7 per cent instead of the previously reported three-tenths of 1 per cent. "This false signal of economic strength in 1984's fourth quarter played a role in the spurt of the dollar to astronomical levels that took place in early 1985," says Robert Barbera, an economist with E. F. Hutton. . . . "The faulty data even fooled the Fed into limiting monetary expansion last year. . . . Before you sit down and make a decision, you want to have the clearest possible assessment of where you are, whether you are an economist, entrepreneur or riverboat gambler."

Labor force statistics—on unions, wages, pension plans, health plans, unemployment—suffered many inadequacies, though they affected important policy questions.

The definition of poverty, adopted more than 25 years ago, became inadequate and did not permit ready analysis of government policies.

An important picture of American business and industry, the Standard Industrial Classification, had not been updated since 1972 and failed to take account of either new industry or the fast-growing service economy. The document retained a code for extraction of pine gum but had none for computer manufacture.

The Census Bureau's monthly trade statistics, and the way they were collected, were overwhelmed by a flood of imports, with the bad trade numbers distorting other key statistics such as the GNP. Imports were not being reported in the month they arrived, and often they were reported many months later. The figures were being collected "largely by hand in customs houses"—"another system," said one economist, "that only Charles Dickens could love."

None of the above means that all government statistics are bad or unreliable. Many are well collected and well analyzed, and for many (by no means all) of the above problems, corrective steps have been belatedly started. Agencies like the Census Bureau, Bureau of Labor Statistics, and National Center for Health Statistics continue to set high standards. Still, there have been problems even in those sterling agencies, and the highly respected BLS commissioner, Janet Norwood, said of the whole federal statistical picture, "As both a producer and consumer of federal statistics, I have found some of these budget cuts extremely painful. The cuts have eliminated or sharply reduced a number of very useful statistical series."

Beyond that, said the critics, "planning for the future, research on new methods and techniques, and recruitment and training of future leadership are increasingly inadequate." The budget cuts had caused high turnover and increasing attrition rates, with "talented young people . . . less willing to enter or continue service in the federal statistical system."

The Bottom Line

The emphasis in this manual has necessarily been on the ways statistics can go wrong, the ways scientific studies can go wrong, the ways reporting can go wrong. If you've read the entire manual, you may decide to believe nothing you hear. That would be what statisticians call a Type II error: failing to detect a result when one is there, or, in practical terms, disbelieving the truth. Believing everything would be a Type I error: believing untruth.

All testing, including a reporter's testing of truth, involves trade-offs. If you're too gullible, you make too many Type I errors. If you're too skeptical or even cynical—the sad person who believes nothing—you make too many Type II errors.

A cynic might say that this manual will convince journalists that they should believe very little but continue to report everything. We shall see.

Where to Learn More: A Bibliography and Other Sources

Statistics texts and manuals:

Freedman, David, Robert Pisani, and Roger Purves. *Statistics*. New York: W. W. Norton, 1978. A complete, readable, and even entertaining statistics text with many examples and anecdotes and a conversational style.

Leaverton, Paul E. *A Review of Biostatistics: A Program for Self-Instruction.* 2d ed. Boston: Little, Brown, 1978. A course of instruction in 87 concise pages.

Moore, David S. *Statistics: Concepts and Controversies.* 2d ed. New York: W. H. Freeman, 1986. A full-size work that lives up to its blurb: "the heart of statistics with careful explanations and real-life examples, avoiding unnecessarily complicated mathematics."

Moses, Lincoln. *Think and Explain With Statistics*. Reading, Mass.: Addison-Wesley, 1986. By a Stanford professor and one of American statistics' major figures. A popular statistics text that is strong on practical use of statistics.

White, David M., and Seymour Levine. *Elementary Statistics for Journalists.* New York: Macmillan, 1954. Professor Michael Greenberg of Rutgers calls this "the best introduction for journalists who have no background nor any time to take a course."

Youden, W. J. *Experimentation and Measurement*. Washington, D.C.: U.S. Government Printing Office, 1984. I'd recommend this as a supplemental source. Written by a consultant to the National Bureau of Standards, it focuses on use of statistics in measurement but also has many valuable sections on statistics in general.

153

Zeisel, Hans. *Say It With Figures.* New York: Harper and Row, 1985.
  6th ed. Both a text and a guide to understanding — and questioning — social statistics.

Epidemiology texts — in fact, simple statistics courses:

Friedman, Gary D. *Primer of Epidemiology.* 3d ed. New York: McGraw-
  Hill, 1987. A Kaiser epidemiologist and biostatistician, Friedman
  covers much of statistics, with examples from medicine and epidemiology. A treasure, concise and easy to read and follow.
Lilienfeld, Abraham, and David E. Lillienfeld. *Foundations of Epidemiology.* 2d ed. New York: Oxford University Press, 1980. A standard,
  for good reason.

*On the statistics of real-life situations — companions to statistics texts and also good
  reading:*

Campbell, Stephen K. *Flaws and Fallacies in Statistical Thinking.* Engle-
  wood Cliffs, N.J.: Prentice-Hall, 1974. The emphasis is on recognizing statistical frauds and whoppers, intentional or otherwise,
  and distinguishing between valid and faulty reasoning.
Huff, Darrell. *How to Lie With Statistics.* New York: W. W. Norton,
  1954. Short, provocative, amusing.
Tanur, Judith M., ed., and by Frederick Mosteller, William H.
  Kruskal, Richard F. Link, Richard S. Pieters, and Gerald R.
  Rising. *Statistics: A Guide to the Unknown.* 2d ed. San Francisco:
  Holden-Day, 1978. An anomaly, a good work produced by a
  committee. This committee was headed by Professor Frederick
  Mosteller. A series of chapters on the practical applications of
  almost every branch of statistics, from surveys to medical experiments to weather to sports.
Vogt, Thomas M. *Making Health Decisions: An Epidemiologic Perspective on
  Staying Well.* Chicago: Nelson-Hall, 1983. For the general reader
  or the journalist, guidance and good reading on "making sound
  judgments about claims and counter-claims" about health and
  disease.

Weaver, Warren. *Lady Luck: The Theory of Probability.* Garden City, N.Y.: Doubleday Anchor Books, 1963. All you want to know about probability, from the amusingly anecdotal to the technical.

On applying statistics and polling methods to reporting:

Meyer, Philip. *Precision Journalism: A Reporter's Introduction to Social Science Methods.* 2d ed. Bloomington: Indiana University Press, 1979. The first and now classic work in this area, by a longtime Detroit Free Press and Knight reporter and editor, now William Rand Kenan, Jr., Professor of Journalism at the University of North Carolina, Chapel Hill.

On statistics in medicine, biomedical research, and clinical trials; written for researchers and physicians but with much rich detail for conscientious medical reporters:

Bailar, John C., III, and Frederick Mosteller, eds. *Medical Uses of Statistics.* Waltham, Mass.: NEJM Books, 1986. This grew out of a series in the *New England Journal of Medicine.*

Inglefinger, J. A., Frederick Mosteller, L. A. Thibodeau, and J. H. Ware. *Biostatistics in Clinical Medicine.* 2d ed. New York: Macmillan, 1986.

Shapiro, Stanley H., and Thomas A. Louis, eds. *Clinical Trials: Issues and Approaches.* New York: Marcel Dekker, 1983.

Warren, Kenneth S. *Coping With the Biomedical Literature: A Primer for the Scientist and the Clinician.* New York: Praeger, 1981.

On health hazards:

Legator, Marvin S., Barbara L. Harper, and Michael J. Scott, eds. *The Health Detective's Handbook: A Guide to the Investigation of Environmental Health Hazards by Nonprofessionals.* Baltimore: Johns Hopkins University Press, 1985. A marvelous practical guide for concerned citizens and inquiring reporters.

Additional resources:

• Any reporter seeking help or interviews on any scientific, medical, technological, environmental, or statistical subject can call the SIPI (Scientists' Institute for Public Information) Media Resource Service at 800–223–1730 toll-free (or in New York State, 212–661–9110), 8:30 A.M. to 7 P.M., Monday through Friday. SIPI will quickly come up with the names and phone numbers of legions of helpful people.

Notes

The full citations to some frequently cited books may be found in the bibliography immediately preceding this section. Unless otherwise indicated, quotations from the following people are from interviews: Drs. John C. Bailar III, Peter Braun, Harvey Fineberg, Thomas A. Louis, Frederick Mosteller, Marvin Zelen, Harvard School of Public Health; H. Jack Geiger, City University of New York; and Arnold Relman, *New England Journal of Medicine*.

Two other important sources for this manual were Drs. Peter Montague, director, Hazardous Waste Research Program, Princeton University, and Michael Greenberg, professor of urban studies and director, Public Policy and Education Hazardous and Toxic Substances Research Center, Rutgers University. Quotations are from their talks at symposiums titled "Public Health and the Environment: The Journalist's Dilemma," which were sponsored by the Council for the Advancement of Science Writing (CASW) at Syracuse University, April 1982; St. Louis, March 1983; and Ohio State University, April 1984.

FOREWORD

1. Jay A. Winsten, "Science and the Media: The Boundaries of Truth," *Health Affairs* (Spring 1985): 5–23.

CHAPTER 1

1. Dorothy Nelkin, background paper in *Science in the Streets: Report of the Twentieth Century Fund Task Force on the Communication of Scientific Risk* (New York: Priority Press, 1984).

2. From many sources on Love Canal, including Marvin S. Legator, "You Can Do It Too," in *Health Detective's Handbook,* ed. Legator, Harper, and Scott.

3. From many sources, including Department of Health and Human Services, National Cancer Institute, *Cancer Prevention Awareness Survey, Technical*

Report, NIH Publication 84-2677, February 1984.

4. Meyer, *Precision Journalism.*

5. "SRP [Savannah River Plant] link to diseases not valid," *Atlanta Journal-Constitution,* 14 August 1983.

6. Vogt, *Making Health Decisions.*

7. Winsten, "Science and the Media."

CHAPTER 2

1. From many news reports, including "Absolutely No Doubt," *Time,* 1 July 1985.

2. "Guidelines for the Cancer-Related Checkup: Recommendations and Rationale," *Ca* (an American Cancer Society journal), July–August, 1980.

3. Marvin Zelen talk at CASW seminar "New Horizons of Science," Cambridge, Mass., November 1982.

4. Vogt, *Making Health Decisions.*

5. John C. Bailar III in *Clinical Trials,* ed. Shapiro and Louis.

6. From many sources, including John T. Bruer, "Methodological Rigor and Citation Frequency in Patient Compliance Literature," *American Journal of Public Health* 72, no. 10 (October 1982): 1119–24; "Despite Guidelines, Many Lung Cancer Trials Poorly Conducted," *Internal Medicine News* (1 January 1984); Rebecca DerSimonian et al., "Reporting on Methods in Clinical Trials," *New England Journal of Medicine* 306, no. 22 (3 June 1982): 1332–37; Kenneth S. Warren in *Coping,* ed. Warren.

7. Friedman, *Primer.*

8. Frederick Mosteller in *Coping,* ed. Warren.

CHAPTER 3

1. Robert Hooke, *How to Tell the Liars From the Statisticians* (New York: Marcel Dekker, 1983).

2. Mosteller talk at CASW seminar "New Horizons of Science."

3. Zelen, "Innovations in the Design of Clinical Trials in Breast Cancer," in *Breast Cancer Research and Treatment,* no. 3 (1983), Proceedings of Fifth Annual San Antonio Breast Cancer Symposium.

4. Friedman, *Primer.*

5. David S. Salsburg, "The Religion of Statistics as Practiced in Medical Journals," *American Statistician* 39, no. 3 (August 1985): 220–22.

6. John Bailar, "Science, Statistics and Deception," *Annals of Internal Medicine* 104, no. 2 (February 1986): 259–60.

7. Vogt, *Making Health Decisions.*

8. Meyer, *Precision Journalism.*

9. J. A. Freiman, cited by Mosteller in *Coping,* ed. Warren.

10. Alvin R. Feinstein, "Epidemiology: Challenges and Controversies," in

1983 Encyclopedia Britannica Medical and Health Annual (Chicago: Encyclopedia Britannica, 1983).

11. David L. Sackett in *Clinical Trials,* ed. Shapiro and Louis.

12. David Hemenway, quoted in a Harvard School of Public Health staff newsletter, November 1983.

13. Thomas Chalmers in *Clinical Trials,* ed. Shapiro and Louis.

14. Horace Freeland Judson, *The Search for Solutions* (New York: Holt, Rinehart and Winston, 1980).

15. Henry K. Beecher, *Measurement of Subjective Responses: Quantitative Effects of Drugs* (New York: Oxford University Press, 1959).

16. Vogt, *Making Health Decisions.*

17. Hooke, *How to Tell the Liars.*

18. Department of Health, Education and Welfare, *The Health Consequences of Smoking: A Report of the Surgeon-General,* 1980.

19. Hooke, *How to Tell the Liars.*

20. Friedman, *Primer.*

21. James Trifel, "Odds are Against Your Beating the Law of Averages," *Smithsonian,* September 1984, 66–75.

22. Friedman, *Primer.*

23. Stephen Jay Gould, "The Median Isn't the Message," *Discover,* June 1985, 40–42.

CHAPTER 4

1. Winsten, "Science and the Media."

2. Thomas Chalmers, quoted in a Harvard School of Public Health staff newsletter, November 1983.

3. Mosteller talk at CASW seminar.

4. Umberto Veronesi, "Cancer Research—Developing Better Clinical Trials," *Therapaeia,* May 1984, 31.

5. "CEA Says Aged Have Attained Economic Parity," *Washington Post,* 6 February 1985.

6. Hooke, *How to Tell the Liars.*

7. Bailar, "Science, Statistics."

8. Salsburg, "Religion of Statistics."

9. Vogt, *Making Health Decisions.*

10. E. Cuyler Hammond, "Smoking in Relation to Death Rates of One Million Men and Women" in *Epidemiological Approaches to the Study of Cancer and Other Chronic Diseases,* ed. W. Haenszel, Department of Health, Education and Welfare, National Cancer Institute Monograph no. 19, January 1986.

11. Eugene D. Robin, *Medical Care Can Be Hazardous to Your Health* (New York: Harper and Row, 1986).

12. Paul Meier, "The Biggest Public Health Experiment Ever," in *Statistics,* ed. Tanur et al.

CHAPTER 5

1. *Morbidity and Mortality Weekly Report* (Centers for Disease Control, Atlanta) 30 (June 1981): 250–52.

2. Vogt, *Making Health Decisions.*

3. Barbara McNeil, et al., "On the Elicitation of Preferences for Alternative Therapies," *New England Journal of Medicine* 306, no. 21 (27 May 1982): 1259–62.

4. David Sackett in *Coping,* ed. Warren.

5. Warren Burkett, *News Reporting: Science, Medicine and High Technology* (Ames, Iowa: Iowa State University Press, 1986).

6. Hammond, "Smoking."

7. Mosteller talk at CASW seminar.

8. Bailar, "Science, Statistics."

9. Robert Boruch, quoted in "Taking the Measure, or Mismeasure, of It All," *New York Times,* August 28, 1984.

10. Arnold Relman in *Clinical Trials,* ed. Shapiro and Louis.

11. Sackett in *Clinical Trials,* ed. Shapiro and Louis.

CHAPTER 6

1. Robin, *Medical Care.*

2. Barbara G. Valanis and Carol S. Perlman, "Home Pregnancy Tests: Prevalence of Use, False-Negative Rates and Compliance With Instructions," *American Journal of Public Health* 72, no. 9 (September 1982): 1034–36.

3. Friedman, *Primer.*

4. Anthony L. Komaroff, "Variability and Inaccuracy of Medical Data," *Proceedings of the IEEE* 67, no. 9 (September 1979): 1200–1203.

5. John Urquhart and Klaus Heilman, *Risk Watch: The Odds of Life* (New York: Facts on File, 1984).

6. Friedman, *Primer.*

7. Interdisciplinary Panel on Carcinogenicity, "Criteria for Evidence of Chemical Carcinogenicity," *Science* 225 (17 August 1984): 682–87.

CHAPTER 7

The information in the section "Reporting Hospital Death Rates" is based in part on an April 1987 health executive training program sponsored by the American Medical Review Research Center and on a paper and sample questions I prepared. Among speakers whose knowledge I drew on were Andrew Webber, American Medical Peer Review Organization; and Drs. Robert Brook, University of California at Los Angeles and Rand Corporation; John Bunker, Stanford Medical Center; Mark Chassin, Rand Corporation; Carlos Enriquez, Peer Review Organization of New Jersey; Sanford Feldman and

William Moncrief, Jr., California Medical Review, Inc.; Harold Luft, University of California at San Francisco; Marilyn Moon, American Association of Retired Persons; Helen Smits, University of Connecticut; and Sidney Wolfe, Public Citizen Health Research Group.

1. In part from Vogt, *Making Health Decisions.*

2. Friedman, *Primer.*

3. In part from John C. Bailar III and Elaine M. Smith, "Progress Against Cancer?" *New England Journal of Medicine* 314, no. 19 (8 May 1986): 1226–32.

4. Primarily from "Comments on the Article by Bailar and Smith, Adapted From the National Cancer Institute Advisory Board Meeting of 19 May 1986," unpublished National Cancer Institute document, 3 June 1986.

5. Earl S. Pollack, "Tracking Cancer Trends: Incidence and Survival," *Hospital Practice* (August 1984): 99–116.

6. Bruce N. Ames, "Dietary Carcinogens and Anti-Carcinogens," *Science* 221, no. 4617 (23 September 1983): 1256–64; Ames, "The Apocalyptics by Edith Efron" (review), *Science 84* (July 1984): 98–99; Ames, quoted in "War on Cancer Aims at Natural Toxins in Health Foods," *Chicago Tribune,* August 29, 1984.

7. Devra Lee Davis, Kenneth Bridbord, and Marvin Schneiderman, "Estimating Cancer Causes: Problems in Methodology, Production and Trends," *Quantification of Occupational Cancer,* Banbury Report no. 9 (Cold Spring Harbor Laboratory, Cold Spring Harbor, N.Y., 1981), 285–316.

CHAPTER 8

1. "Can Science Deal With Environmental Uncertainties," *Conservation Foundation Letter,* January 1982.

2. Dr. Genevieve Matanoski, Johns Hopkins University, in talk at conference titled "Toxics and the News," sponsored by the Foundation for American Communications and the Gannett Foundation, Princeton, N.J., May 1984.

3. B. B. Cohen et al., *Environmental Health: A Plan for Collecting and Coordinating Statistical and Epidemiologic Data* (National Center for Health Statistics, Government Printing Office, Washington, D.C., 1980).

4. William H. Inman, director, Drug Surveillance Unit, University of Southampton, "Risks in Medical Intervention," Wolfson College lecture, Oxford, 31 January 1984.

5. Barbara S. Hulka, "When Is the Evidence for 'No Association' Sufficient?" (editorial), *Journal of the American Medical Association* 252, no. 1 (6 July 1984): 811–12.

6. William D. Ruckelshaus, quoted in "Risk-Benefit Analysis Is Key Tool in U.S. Regulation of Chemicals," *Washington Post,* 3 January 1985.

7. Nelkin, background paper; and *Science in the Streets.*

8. Jean Mayer and Jeanne Goldberg, "Nutrition" (weekly column), *Washington Post,* 19 August 1984.

9. Vogt, *Making Health Decisions.*

10. From numerous news reports in 1986 and 1987.

11. Rodger Pirnie Doyle, *The Medical Wars* (New York: William Morrow, 1983).

12. Gary D. Friedman, personal communication.

13. David Harris, "Health Department: Enemy or Champion of the People?" (editorial), *American Journal of Public Health* 74, no. 5 (May 1984): 428–30.

14. Hooke, *How to Tell the Liars.*

15. Statistics on risks in this section are from Urquhart and Heilman, *Risk Watch;* Air Transport Association of America; and Insurance Institute for Highway Safety.

16. Douglas R. Hofstadter, *Mathematical Themas* (New York: Basic Books, 1985).

17. Jim Detjen talk at CASW seminars "Public Health and the Environment."

18. Nelkin, background paper.

CHAPTER 9

Among those testifying or otherwise speaking in the section on faulty federal statistics are the following: James Bonnen, Michigan State University, 1978–80 director, President's Reorganization Project for the Federal Statistical System (a study that was filed and ignored); Joseph Duncan, chief economist, Dun and Bradstreet, 1978–81 director, Office of Management and Budget's federal statistical policy coordinating office (thereafter largely dismantled); Ruth Hanft, 1977–81 deputy assistant secretary for health, Department of Health, Education and Welfare; F. Thomas Juster, director, Institute for Social Research, University of Michigan; I. Richard Savage, Yale University; Courtenay Slater, 1977–81 chief economist, Commerce Department, and author of another federally commissioned study on government statistics; Samuel Thier, president, Institute of Medicine–National Academy of Sciences; Katherine Wallman, executive director, Council of Professional Associations on Federal Statistics, former OMB and Commerce official; and Gail Wilensky, vice president, health affairs, Project Hope, and 1975–83 senior research manager, National Center for Health Services Research.

1. Florence Nightingale, quoted by Mark Kac in "Marginalia: Florence Nightingale Among the Statisticians," *American Scientist* 72 (January-February 1984): 72–73.

2. Huff, *How to Lie.*

3. Nancy Lyon Spruill, "Perspective: Politics by the Numbers," *Washington Post,* 20 September 1984.

4. "Meat Export Rise Could Buoy Prices," *Washington Post,* 31 March 1973.

5. "Navy's Cost Claims on Planes Are Hit," *Washington Post,* 28 July 1986.

6. Daniel Seligman, "We're Drowning in Phony Statistics," *Fortune,* November 1961.

7. Robert Samuelson, "The Joy of Statistics," *Newsweek,* 4 November 1985.

8. From several articles, including "Elderly Not on 'Easy Street,' Foundation Study Concludes," *Washington Post,* 22 January 1987; "Despite Gains, 13% of Elderly Live in Poverty, Study Finds," *New York Times,* 31 March 1987.

9. Janet Norwood talk at National Academy of Sciences conference titled "Health Care in America: Reconciling Costs and Quality," 6 April 1987.

10. Clyde H. Farnsworth, "The Government's Statistics—Oranges, Tangerines and Politics," *New York Times,* 1 September 1987.

11. Robert Samuelson, "False Signals on Inflation," *Newsweek,* 28 July 1986.

12. I. Richard Savage, presidential address, American Statistical Association, Philadelphia, 14 August 1984.

13. "How the Poll Was Conducted," *New York Times,* 9 January 1987.

14. Louis Harris, quoted on National Public Radio, 8 November 1984.

15. Richard Wirthlin, quoted in "Public Opinion Polls: Are They Science or Art?" Los Angeles Times–Washington Post News Service, 27 August 1984.

16. Samuelson, "Joy of Statistics."

17. Shere Hite, *Women and Love: A Cultural Revolution in Progress* (New York: Alfred A. Knopf, 1987); Sally Squires, "Modern Couples Say They're Happy Together," *Washington Post,* 27 October 1987; David Streitfeld, "Shere Hite and the Trouble With Numbers," *Washington Post,* 10 November 1987; "Hite Lacks Depth, Says Rival Poll," *New York Daily News,* 29 October 1987; Arlie Russell Hochschild, "Why Can't a Man Be More Like a Woman?" *New York Times Book Review,* 15 November 1987; "Men Aren't Her Only Problem," *Newsweek,* 23 November 1987.

18. Julian L. Simon, "Probability—'Batter's Slump' and Other Illusions," *Washington Post,* 9 August 1987.

19. Mosteller, personal communication.

20. Hooke, *How to Tell the Liars.*

21. Huff, *How to Lie.*

22. "U.S. Whites 10 Times Wealthier Than Blacks, Census Study Finds," *New York Times;* UPI dispatch; and "Wide Racial Disparities Found in Household Wealth," *Washington Post;* 19 July 1986. "Now, a Black Wealth Gap," *Newsweek,* 28 July 1986.

23. Ralph Kinney Bennett, *Reader's Digest,* interview with author.

24. "Deaths in Building-Site Accidents Found to Be Highest in New York," *New York Times,* 21 September 1987.

25. Joseph L. Gastwirth, "Statistically, AIDS Poses Significant Risk" (letter to editor), *New York Times,* 1 July 1987.

26. Stephen G. Pauker, and Klemens B. Meyer, "Screening for HIV: Can We Afford the False Positive Rate?" *New England Journal of Medicine* 317, no. 4 (23 July 1987): 238–41; Susan Okie, "AIDS 'False Positives': A Volatile Social Issue," *Washington Post,* 23 July 1987.

27. Panel on Occupational Safety and Health Statistics (Seymour Geisser, chairman), *Counting Injuries and Illnesses in the Workplace: Proposals for a Better System* (Washington, D.C.: National Research Council, 1987).

Glossary / Index

Glossary terms appear below in **boldface type.**

ABC News poll, of Hite report findings, 140

Absolute survival (or observed survival): The actual proportion of a group alive after a certain period, often compared with relative survival, 87. *See also* **Relative survival**

Accidents, automobile and airline, 122–23

Accuracy
of survey answers, 52
of tests, 64, 66. *See also* **Validity**

Acquired Immune Deficiency Syndrome (AIDS), 44, 46, 50, 72, 144–45

Actuarial method, 87. *See also* **Life table method**

Adjusted rate (or standardized rate): A way of comparing two groups that differ in some important variable (e.g., age) by mathematically eliminating the effect of that variable, 77, 78

Age, as a confounder, 28

Agent Orange, 44

Aggregate numbers, 134

Aging, and cancer mortality, 92–93. *See also* Elderly

AIDS. *See* Acquired Immune Deficiency Syndrome

Air standards, 117

Alderman, Jeff, 140

Alper, Philip, 74

Alpha error, 22. *See also* **False positive**

Alzheimer's disease, 35–36, 96

American Cancer Society
recommendation for Pap smear, 9
smoking and lung cancer study, 46
statistics, 88

American Journal of Public Health, 121

American Medical Review Research Center, 160

Ames, Bruce, 94

Ames test, 94

Analytic study: An observational study that seeks to analyze or explain the occurrence of a disease or characteristic in a population, 44

Anecdotes, limitations of, 19, 37–38, 49, 131

Animals, as research subjects, 72–73

Annual Cancer Statistics Reviews (NCI), 89

Aristotle, on probability, 14

Asbestos, and smoking, 28

Association
hidden, 41
noncausal, 17, 54, 85
questions about, 54–56, 111
specific, 56
spurious, 24
strength of, 108